Praise f

The seven "Warriors with Character" represent the true character of the majority who serve in today's Armed Services and are the strength of this nation. This book shows that in dealing with their life-threatening injuries, they have had to manifest resilience, toughness, positive thinking, as well as tenderness and reflection. The stories also point out the important role that family and loved ones play in the successful rehabilitation of our severely wounded service members.

Having had the honor of knowing three of the warriors, Justin, Todd, and Sam, who have gone through Disabled Sports USA's Warfighter Sports Rehabilitation program, I can attest to the true character of these fine "Warfighters." I am also delighted with Brad's performance through our partner, USA Paralympics, in winning one silver and two gold medals in the Summer Paralympics in London! His performance was a shining example of the value of sport in rehabilitation.

—Kirk M. Bauer, J.D., U.S. Army (Ret.)
Executive Director, Disabled Sports USA

This is an important book for all Americans, especially our youth. They need to know the difference between celebrities and true heroes—that difference being goodness, which is essential for a true hero. Despite inequality in ability and opportunity, young people should know they can have all the courage they want, they can't use it up, and courage is the key to success in life. God makes courage infinitely available to all, and it destroys all excuses for failure and mediocrity, stamping them as the result of choice, not chance. This book identifies true heroes and highlights the incredible fruits of courage.

—Congressional Medal of Honor Recipient, Major General Pat Brady
U.S. Army (Ret.)

Courage in America: Warriors with Character is the premier book covering the other side of combat: life for our returning wounded. This book chronicles sailors, soldiers, and Marines as they patrol the streets facing fear and fighting the enemy. When tragedy strikes and these warriors are life-flighted from the battlefield to hospitals, we join them bedside as they struggle with the gains and setbacks of recovery. In their own words, they detail the physical, mental, emotional, and spiritual hurdles encountered during their rehabilitation and explain how their training and moral compass guided them on this life-altering journey. Kerrigan beautifully weaves their vignettes and the guiding principles that inspire them to serve and galvanize a successful reintegration. In an age where society needs a hero, this wholesome and uplifting book introduces us to seven humble men and the loved ones who supported them in their darkest hour.

—*Captain Aloysius Boyle, U.S. Marine Corps (Ret.), Company Commander Wounded Warrior Battalion—East Walter Reed Army Medical Center National Naval Medical Center, Bethesda*

You owe it to YOURSELF to read these stories. These warriors learned critical life lessons in the hardest way and at great personal cost. They are now sharing them with you and it costs you only a couple hours of your time. What a bargain… Bravo Zulu, Mike. Semper Fi.

—*Tom Esslinger, Chief Operating Officer, Marine Corps Association & Foundation; Commanding Officer, Mike Company, 3rd Battalion, 26th Marines on Hill 881S outside Khe Sanh Combat Base during the Tet Offensive in 1968*

What's truly remarkable about the narratives of *Courage in America: Warriors with Character* is how unremarkable the storytellers consider courage to be. For these seven soldiers, Marines, and sailor, courage takes many forms: having the conviction to enlist, showing bravery in battle, surviving the unimaginable, and every day, despite wounds that will never heal, pressing on. It's impossible to understand what courage actually means until you are forced to tap into it—and thanks to the sacrifices of veterans like these, most of us won't ever need to. For all of us fortunate enough to never know bravery in our own lives, *Courage in America: Warriors with Character* should be required reading.

—*Karen Guenther, Founder and CEO of Semper Fi Fund*

Courage in America: Warriors with Character is an incredibly powerful compilation of individual stories that detail the extreme challenges and harrowing nature of combat, but this book is much more than that. These are stories of ordinary young men who were shaped by their experiences in the military, on the battlefield, and through agonizing recoveries associated with traumatic and tragic wounds. They became extraordinary in the process.

These warriors have remarkable stories to tell, and Mike Kerrigan does a great job of capturing the warrior ethos of our war fighters and the personal courage of each who contributed their story. They have insight and wisdom that can only be gained in the crucible of battle. What makes this offering unique and invaluable is the application of this insight and wisdom through their discussion on courage in the second half of the book. These are powerful life lessons that were gained the hard way and are now available to us all.

—*Randy Hammond, Lieutenant Colonel U.S. Marine Corps (Ret.)*
Awarded the Distinguished Flying Cross for Valor in Desert Storm

Courage in America: Warriors with Character is a well-overdue glimpse into the experiences of our wounded warriors. Much more than just war stories, Michael Kerrigan's powerful work provides us seven faces to go with the expression "the hotter the flame, the harder the steel" while providing much-needed lessons in character for our nation.

—*Lieutenant Colonel Eric Holt, D.O.*
Air Force Special Operations Command

Fantastic book. Today, approximately one-half of one percent of all Americans serve in the military at any given time, and as the size of our military shrinks, there is a bigger and bigger disconnect between American civilians and our military. It's too easy to forget about those few brave men and women who sacrifice so much for our country. *Courage in America: Warriors with Character,* through the personal stories told in their own words, reminds us of the sacrifices these American heroes make for us every day. Thanks, Mike, for bringing these stories to us. We must never forget.

—Steve McCullough, U.S. Marine Corps (Ret.)
Served in Vietnam assigned to 11th Interrogation & Translation Team, MACV, I Corps
Awarded Bronze Star with "V" for Combat Valor
Vietnam Armed Forces Honor Medal
Navy Unit Citation

Courage in America: Warriors with Character brings to light these brave heroes' amazing stories of resilience and of overcoming adversity. Readers will relate to how their stories began, and will be humbled and awestruck by the extraordinary sacrifices they and others have made for our freedom. Every American should read this book.

—Captain Jim Nemec, Operation Iraqi Freedom (05-06), (08-09)
Operation Enduring Freedom (11-12)

The "American Experiment" has been challenged, assaulted, and debated for over 236 years now, but still stands, and has stood, the test of time. More capitals today emulate it worldwide than ever. Life does not look back, but if our forefathers could have seen our destiny, they would have said that it is because of the courage, drive, commitment, and character of young men and women like these seven whom Michael Kerrigan has so masterfully described in his superb new book, *Courage in America: Warriors with Character.* It is this passion and strength to succeed at all cost that puts the great individuals in the forefront of the American spirit. Read this book slowly and share it with your children.

—Tommy Norman, Chairman, Charlotte Bridge Home

Michael Kerrigan's book *Courage in America: Warriors with Character* continues President Abraham Lincoln's legacy with firm resolve to not only honor, but also to remember, those who have served, and those who have returned as wounded warriors. In reading this book, we meet several warriors, and we learn their combat stories. We learn of their courage, their strength, and their wounds. They have invaluable lessons to share. To these warriors, we must pay homage. We must extend the rallying cry to all Americans, and reinforce the message that in our daily lives, we are free to pursue our liberties because of the mighty protection provided by our U.S. Military. *Courage in America: Warriors with Character* is inspiration to be shared with every American.

—Jennifer Pinto, Vice President
Managing Director, Marketing
Swett & Crawford, New York

When one visits Walter Reed, you aren't sure how you will respond to people whose bodies have been torn apart. However, what you see are the strongest, bravest, and most motivated people you will ever meet. Mike Kerrigan has captured that spirit with the stories in *Courage in America: Warriors with Character.* It makes you proud to know these young men and women, and to know what courage looks like up close and personal.

—Mark E. Robbins, CAE, Executive Director,
Yellow Ribbon Fund

Courage in America: Warriors with Character is more than "merely" the inspiring story of seven wounded warriors overcoming their injuries through determined, relentless hard work, shared love, and the dedication of loved ones. Todd, Chase, Brad, Sam, Steven, Justin, and Chad share their stories in their own words. Honest, clear-eyed, patriotic, these men tell of the events that prepared them for the challenges they have come to face. *Courage in America: Warriors with Character* becomes more than an inspiring set of stories because we are allowed to see these wounded warriors in the moments, months, and years since their injuries: their moments of doubt, their decisions to overcome adversity, yes, their hard physical work, but really and most genuinely, their DECISION to fight back and excel. Adaptability. Resiliency. Courage. Discipline. Hard work. Fortitude. Gumption. These are the arrows in the quiver of life-tools. The challenges are extreme, but their mind-set is the key. These life-tools are available to everyone, which is what makes this book universal. We all face difficult moments. Will we be broken or tempered? These men's stories illuminate the path of hope for themselves and for all of us. Read the book and realize that even when fate wounds us or causes us to stumble, there is a path that leads to a better life. Thank you, Michael Kerrigan, for ensuring that these seven brave warriors have a chance to share their life lessons.

—*Lieutenant Commander Eric Rubenstein, Ph.D.*
U.S. Navy

I have had the privilege of visiting our military hospitals multiple times here and abroad and have met the most courageous individuals I have ever known. The seven stories in *Courage in America: Warriors with Character* are shining examples of some of the extraordinary warriors who motivate me each day to continue the work on behalf of our men and women in uniform. I urge you to read this book. I know you will be moved by the inspirational stories of the courage and character of these great Americans.

—*Gary Sinise, Actor*
Founder, Gary Sinise Foundation

By their actions in combat, the men in this book replicated courage as described by Plato in *The Republic*. Plato wrote that courage is essential to go to war, and that wisdom is necessary to know that courage must have an element of moderation. If not, courage carried too far, becomes brutality. These men showed true courage.

—*Congressional Medal of Honor Recipient, Colonel Leo K. Thorsness*
U.S. Air Force (Ret.)

Courage in America

Warriors with Character

MICHAEL J. KERRIGAN

Published by Wheatmark˙
1760 East River Road, Suite 145
Tucson, Arizona 85718 U.S.A.
www.wheatmark.com

Paperback ISBN: 978-1-60494-872-1
Hardcover ISBN: 978-1-60494-873-8
Ebook ISBN: 978-1-60494-874-5

LCCN: 2012950466

rev201201

Then will he strip his sleeve and show his scars,
And say 'These wounds I had on Crispin's day.'
Old men forget; yet all shall be forgot,
But he'll remember with advantages
What feats he did that day. Then shall our names
Familiar in his mouth as household words—
Harry the king, Bedford and Exeter,
Warwick and Talbot, Salisbury and Gloucester—
Be in their flowing cups freshly remember'd.
This story shall the good man teach his son;
And Crispin Crispian shall ne'er go by,
From this day to the ending of the world,
But we in it shall be remember'd;
We few, we happy few, we band of brothers;
For he today that sheds his blood with me
Shall be my brother; be he ne'er so vile,
This day shall gentle his condition;
And gentlemen in England now a-bed
Shall think themselves accursed they were not here,
And hold their manhoods cheap whiles any speaks
That fought with us upon Saint Crispin's day.

—William Shakespeare, *Henry V, Scene III*
Speech to rally warriors in the English camp

Dedication

204th Area Support Medical Company returning home from Iraq
(Photo Credit: Sgt. Dajon N. Schafer, Minnesota National Guard Public Affairs)

I dedicate this book to our nation's wounded warriors who are returning home scarred from battle, often without limbs, without sight, or without relief from post-traumatic stress. With this publication, I wish to thank them for their service and to make sure their sacrifices are not forgotten. Many have paid dearly for their patriotism. This book also salutes their heroic caregivers: the moms, dads, wives, husbands, siblings, friends, medics, corpsmen, and health care professionals who sacrifice daily to provide loving support for the injured.

Acknowledgements

I would like to salute Sam Angert, Steve Baskis, Justin Constantine, Chase Cooper, Chad Ellinger, Todd Nicely, and Brad Snyder–the seven warriors whose stories are life examples of good character in action. I appreciate their willingness to inspire other wounded warriors to persevere in their recoveries. Their constant and active participation in this project has given a voice to many other warriors like them. Each has helped us all to better understand what they do in combat and what keeps them fighting through the long battle of rehabilitation.

I would like to acknowledge the families of the wounded warriors whom I visited for their willingness to give me a glimpse of what is involved in rebuilding an injured warrior's life. They did so in the hope that their successes can help other warrior families hang tough and get through the long path to recovery.

I also must recognize the crucial role of the medical caregivers: the medics, corpsmen, nurses, doctors, surgeons, psychologists, physical and occupational therapists. The warriors highlighted in this book would not have recovered without their unwavering dedication. These health professionals jumped into action from the moment of traumatic injury, shepherding the warriors through multiple medical procedures, and on through the occupational and psychological support services needed later. Amidst demanding hospital schedules, they continue to help me to capture stories of successful recoveries.

Turning to the mechanics of production, I wish to thank my publisher, Sam Henrie, and his editorial and design team at Wheatmark. Sam's critical advice has greatly improved the manuscript, and he kept publication on schedule. I also wish to thank Paul Stoltz, Ph.D., for his mentoring about understanding adversity, a topic he has spent a career dissecting. Paul's generous conversations with me better prepared me to interact helpfully with the wounded warriors. And my gratitude ever extends to Donna Kerrigan, my wife of 44 years, for her longstanding support for all my professional endeavors, including *Courage in America: Warriors with Character,* the latest product of The Character Building Project.

All profits from the sale of *Courage in America: Warriors with Character* will be donated to financially sound charitable organizations whose mission is to help wounded warriors.

Contents

Foreword

by Paul Stoltz, Ph.D.

Courage.

Read that word slowly. Let it take residence inside of you.

What two syllables can more concisely and profoundly determine the destiny of our world, or of a single human life? And what seven letters can more readily challenge, spark and elevate one's best, both on and off the battlefield?

This wake-up call of a book honors not just the seven warriors it highlights, but it brings to life all whom must somehow summon and sustain courage in the face of the most unspeakable fears and overwhelming adversities, for a noble cause.

Through these soul-stirring stories, *Courage in America* also implicitly confronts us with some profound questions: What is your personal relationship with courage? What role has courage played in shaping you, your path, your life, and your aspirations? And what does the soul-soaring word "courage" really mean?

Chase, Justin, Chad, Steve, Sam, Todd, and Brad teach us that the same virtues that lead to success in battle are what sustain us through life's travails. So, if you think this book is only for and about soldiers, our warriors at war, you are absolutely wrong. If you think this book is ultimately for and about you—about everyone's and anyone's opportunity to dig deeply and be more—then you have already begun to understand the deep marrow of this book.

Before you turn to the next page, beware. If this book came with a warning label, it would say: Don't read on unless you are prepared to be humbled to near tears, jarred out of complacency, and spurred to do more first, in every encounter with anyone who has served their country, and second, in your own journey with courage.

These warriors' stories, like all stories of courage have a common element, adversity. Without it, courage means nothing. Courage is only courage and virtue is only virtue when tested by adversity. And if adversity is defined as "Experiencing something bad happening to someone or something you care about," then the worse it is, and the more you care, the greater the adversity.

That is part of what makes *Courage in America* such an important read. It reveals to us how courage is everything, especially when smacked with potentially catastrophic adversity. It invites you to consider your own relationship with adversity and ask what courage you could better muster to carve a noble path forward.

This book awakens us to the many forms of courage, and how different they are from each other. The courage to step up, volunteer is one thing. The courage to face evil is another. The courage to suffer and endure is entirely different. But in the end, they are all courage in the face of adversity, which is the only time courage matters.

In an airport recently, I watched as a businessman averted his eyes when some uniformed troops passed by to board the plane. He looked uncomfortable. I told him I couldn't help noticing, and asked him why he looked away. He responded, "It's just that I never know what to say. I mean, it's so weird, them off fighting for our country, and I'm here, flying around selling IT solutions. It's like two different worlds, ya know?" Yeah, I know.

Michael Kerrigan, in writing this book, reminds us, it's time to stop looking away, and look our soldiers—our men and women in uniform—straight in the heart and in the eye, and say, "Thank you. Thank you for the courage you've had to show to do what you've done and do what you do, just so we can go to bed safe and secure, with our flag flying high."

Kerrigan writing on courage? You may be wondering why this recovering Washington lobbyist, Michael Kerrigan, would take on this subject and such a noble quest. After spending countless hours in deep conversation with the author, I can tell you it is for one reason.

Kerrigan wrote this book for you because he cares. His is not a "This subject is really important to me," kind of care. Rather, this is Michael's "If I could move the needle on one single aspect of our society before I die, this must be it, and I can't sleep until I do" kind of care. He cares about strengthening America's character the way you and I care about finding air to breathe in an overcrowded subway. He fears with the current course unaltered, America's character may dwindle, and he wants to do his part to replenish our supply.

As you read these warriors' courageous stories, don't forget to shift this book into a mirror. For one of Kerrigan's main lessons is one of my favorite quotes: "It is in the flames of adversity that our character is forged."

Paul Stoltz, Ph.D. is the originator of Adversity Quotient® (AQ®) and the world's leading expert on the subject. He founded PEAK Learning® in 1987 and now works with top leaders and thinkers worldwide within a broad range of organizations ranging from startups to NGOs to the Fortune 100. Dr. Stoltz oversees research in 17 countries. His partners include thought leaders at Yale University, Stanford University, and more than a dozen universities overseas. Hailed by Executive Excellence as "one of the 100 most influential thinkers of our time," Dr. Stoltz is a member of Stanford University's Distinguished Leaders Lecture Series.

Introduction

*C*ourage in America began as part of my service project as a member of The Knights of Malta, a Roman Catholic service organization. I visited wounded warriors at Walter Reed Hospital in Washington, D.C., and later, at Walter Reed National Military Medical Center in Bethesda, Maryland, and Fort Belvoir, Virginia, where I focused my attention on extraordinary young Americans who volunteered for military service in response to the attack on America on September 11, 2001 and afterward.

By presenting to you the stories of seven wounded warriors whom I met during my volunteer work, I hope to highlight the courage that enables them, and military heroes like them, to turn the extreme adversity of war and its injuries into a successful recovery and re-entry into civilian life.

Originally I set out to examine the virtue of courage in our nation's warriors: how it is taught, practiced, and sustained among the young generation of Americans in the military. By volunteering to help the wounded among them, I discovered something unexpected. There was no need to examine men in battle to understand courage. All that was needed was to visit the sick and injured at Walter Reed National Military Medical Center and Ft. Belvoir. There many young lives lie in hospital beds suffering with war wounds. Patients recovering from traumatic injury know that it often takes more courage to live than to die, and yet still these young men and women chose to carry on. Propelled by courage, they are determined to rebuild their lives and recover as fully as possible.

My visits with the wounded warriors left me wondering just what enables a young person, an 18-year-old high-school graduate to join the military, find himself or herself in a combat zone, and be able to run toward the gunfire when commanded to do so? And an even more puzzling question was what gave these young warriors, after returning home, the courage to successfully rebuild body, mind, soul, and world? I wondered if it is possible for a warrior with courage in battle to exhaust his or her courage and be defeated in rehabilitation? Can courage be trained into a young warrior or is it in the genes? Is courage shaped at an early age, or does it develop with maturity and military training? Why do some navigate their recovery so exceptionally well and find meaning in their suffering, while other warriors become victims? How do the successful ones become masters of themselves and not victims of their emotions, particularly fear?

The overarching answer seems to lie in the warrior's ability to muster courage as needed in his soul.

What follow are the stories of seven men who did just that. At their core, they have demonstrated courage in combat and in the longer battle of rehabilitation. The stories are their own explanations of how they conquered what happened. In recounting their military experiences, they explore what they felt before departure, during war, and during their recovery process.

I hope that listening to the voices of these representative wounded warriors will provide helpful insights to many. Looking into the lives of a few young men who sacrificed much for their country should be an invaluable read for high school graduates who are considering a military career. The narratives should also give college-bound students an appreciation for the sacrifices made by some of their high school classmates. College students will readily realize that while they were enjoying campus life, some of their contemporaries were learning much outside the classroom—lessons from war—like the value of honor, perseverance, selflessness, patience, resilience, and endurance. And all readers will be touched by the resolve of loving families from small towns across our country who rally around their injured loved ones and endure along with them until recovery is complete.

By sharing these stories of warriors and their caregivers, I hope to inspire the newly wounded to take heart and reach for the fullest recovery possible. Although their circumstances may not be identical to those described in this book, hopefully, they are similar enough to inspire belief in recovery.

It is an honor to give voice to the military who are recovering from traumatic injuries. They achieve greatness of character each day by harnessing adversity and overcoming their injuries. Some remain "works in progress," but all are climbing in a positive way toward everyday greatness. They are the living embodiment of a noble military tradition of high-minded service.

In Their Own Words

Their Stories

Sam's Story

This tale goes as far back as I can remember. I am not sure whether it is based my own recall, or I am retelling the stories that were told to me, but this is what I've experienced and made my own during the past 23 years. I need to tell this story, if only to myself. I feel that way because I think that everyone in life has something to tell, something to contribute, especially when he or she have faced adversity well. I hope that by telling my story of recovery from traumatic war injuries, I can help others who face similar adversity.

I was born Samuel Michael Angert on July 13, 1989. My grandparents brought my mother Polina and her brother Gary to the United States in 1979. My mother was 8 years old when she arrived, and Gary was about to turn age 18. My grandfather, Mikhail Riter, was a young retired military who jumped with the airborne division in Russia. He was one of many courageous men who chose to take their families and move away from the Union of Soviet Socialist Republics. Before any of them were able to even enter the United States, there were some things that needed to be done. Having a contact in America at that time was a crucial factor in making the move successful. So because he was a very tactical individual, my grandfather thought it wise to make a pit stop in Italy so that a smooth entry could be made into the United States.

Late in the year 1979, my family got settled in Brooklyn, New York. This to them was the land of opportunity with so many chances for success, but the options were limited for people who had just immigrated to the country. Money was scarce for my family, as it was for everyone in our neighborhood in the early '80s.

At that time, my mother had met a man by the name of Vladimir Angert. Being young, naïve, and in need of help, she hit it off with him and soon began to date. Before you knew it, they were married. By the time my first birthday celebration came along, my grandparents noticed that Vlad was a very wild young man. Unfortunately Vlad got caught up making runs for the Italians in Brooklyn. The money was good, life was good, but as a father, he was unreliable, and as a husband, even more careless and disappointing. My mom had given him many chances to straighten up, but he continued to disappoint her.

Making runs for the Italians in Brooklyn in the early '90s was definitely a serious business. My uncle Gary was later recruited by Vlad to make runs with him in and out of state. The situation was bad. The Feds were bringing the heat, and they let the neighborhood know that whoever was living the high life based upon that racket (namely, making runs for the mob) would get caught and do federal time eventually. They were right. Nothing lasts forever. So my uncle cut the runs short and gave up on it. In June 1990, he and his wife brought my beautiful little cousin Victoria Riter into this world. Uncle Gary changed his line of work and worked hard to support his family, and he did a great job raising his baby girl.

My biological father Vlad was not as wise as Uncle Gary. By the summer of 1990, he had his head so far up his ass on drugs that he didn't see how his actions were tearing our family apart. Not only was he ruining his marriage carelessly, but he was also being a terrible father. He was only around when it was convenient for him. I was too young to remember this, but I think on or around my first birthday, my mother got fed up and left him. She decided that it was about time to get serious and raise her son in the right way. After my mother left Vlad, he got caught up with the Feds, and he served time in prison for quite a while.

Mom was living alone raising me and supporting both of us. From that young age of one, I was left with no father figure, so I became, and remain, mamma's boy. Turning to mom for help was how I operated, and it is something I do even now. I am blessed to have my mother, and I am beyond grateful for how consistently she supports me as a mother and as a dear friend in my life.

The following summer of 1991, for my second birthday, mom took me to the Catskill Mountains where she and my grandparents used to spend time enjoying a summer getaway. Being a little munchkin always giving everyone a hard time, I decided to run away into the middle of the parking lot near the pool area, and as luck would have it, I ran into something. I should say that I thought I ran into something, because I actually ran into the arms of a man named Boris, who liked me immediately, before he even met my mom. He picked me up and, with his two friends beside him, he returned me to my mom, who was running around in a panic looking for her boy on the loose.

As mom tells the story, Boris actually fell in love with me before she even met him. It was like a story from a fairytale. I think it is pretty cool. To all the ladies out there who don't think it is possible to experience love at first sight, I want to say, "Well, believe it, because I am a living proof. " Mom and Boris dated for a little while, then he proposed, and they got married.

Before you knew it, in 1995, mom and Boris brought my little brother into this world. Daniel Jacob Drabkin was a blessing in disguise, although, at first, it was more of a jealousy issue for me. After being the only child for several years—we are 6 years apart in age—I felt the attention was now all on him, and I was not happy. Being too young to understand, I would throw fits. Today I am truly blessed to have Daniel around, and he is always there for whatever the family needs. He will turn age 17 this spring and is captain of his varsity swim team at Lincoln High School in Brooklyn. I am proud of him and always will be. He is a focused young man.

Looking back, I was equally focused at the age of 17. Academic demands at school were never an issue. I played sports, kept myself busy, and was always a family boy. Growing up in Brooklyn, I had to adjust quickly and understand that amidst so many diverse cultures, no one was really that different. At least, that is how I saw it: people are people, some from your own background, and many from different ones. Knowing this as a young boy enabled me to get along and interact well with everyone. Since kindergarten my teachers used to call me a "yenta." In Yiddish, this word is given to someone (usually female) who knows the gossip and talks a lot.

I had an amazing childhood and was never deprived of anything, so I thank my parents for that as well as my grandparents. They all were always there for me and allowed me to experience the childhood that many kids dream of having.

After I finished the eighth grade at the Bay Academy of Arts and Sciences I.S. 98, my dad Boris decided to move our family to the vicinity of Boston, Massachusetts. He was given a business offer in the optical field as a profession. For my brother and me, this new environment was a very rural one compared to Brooklyn. I started my freshman year at Braintree High School, which was in the small town of Braintree. After getting comfortable there my first year, my parents once again up and moved us to another town in the neighboring area. A town called Stoughton. So I finished my high school years and represented the Stoughton Black Knights and joined the graduating class of 2007.

Throughout my high school years, all these recruiters would come to school and speak to high school students about how the military was so great. They would brag to me and my peers about how good life could be if we were joined. As a young man in my teens, I was raised with values of discipline, manners, and respect, so I admired those traits in the military recruiters whom I met.

I started college in September of 2007, but I continued to contemplate joining the military. The discipline and other good characteristics I carried with me from growing up in a good family made me a good young man, in general, but I just felt that I needed someone or something to instill more discipline and good character traits in me on a daily basis. I finished my first semester of college, but I wasn't as focused as I had hoped that I would be. So at the age of 18, before I signed up for my second semester of college, I joined the military after having many long and thorough discussions with my folks.

In January 2008, I set foot on the bus to be "sent out." Just what does that mean? Well, you must understand that because you are an active duty soldier does not mean that you are sent off right away to war or to fight terrorism. More than 90 percent of the time, active duty soldiers are domestic, stationed here in the United States. In that case, "sent out" is just another way of saying, "I'm home training, preparing for whatever is to come in the future, whether it be deployment or more training." The government does their very best and spends a tremendous amount of money so that every soldier is tactically efficient in their military occupation specialties.

Each soldier goes through a basic training process and mine started like this. On the night of February 3, 2008, I stepped off of the bus in Fort Benning, Georgia and was slapped in the face with what I like to call a little taste of bittersweet reality. Within the next few days came nothing but exhaustion, long days, sleep deprivation, getting screamed at by drill instructors, and very little time to relax. This was something that no man, including me, was prepared for either mentally or physically.

Once we were broken down into separate platoons, all I knew was that for the following four months, I would have nothing but the men beside me, and my goal was to stabilize my mind and know that this would all be over soon.

The first few weeks where the roughest, because I was left with two options: either to be friendly with these strangers or not. There were many of the recruits that would let their egos take control, and they thought that how they acted on the outside world was how they were going to act here. I knew being there was going to strip me of any contact I had to the outside world. I was very emotional and homesick, but yet, at the back of my head, I knew that once I was out of here, the tactics and training I learned would do me much good in the long run throughout my military career. I was put to the test physically and mentally the entire time there. I needed to make sure all rules were obeyed and that I was doing the right thing. The drill instructors would

Sam (right) with 2nd Lieutenant Joseph Fortin,
who was killed by the same IED that wounded Sam

tell us, "Private, when you get to your unit, as long as you're at the right place, at the right time, in the right uniform, you will never have any issues."

The first two months went by and things became a bit easier, especially because my fellow recruits and I were becoming much closer. We came to understand, little by little, that no matter how vigorous the training, we needed to pull through this fight together. All these men beside me had signed up to fight for their country, too. To represent the "red white and blue" was everyone's goal. We knew at some point we could all be deployed to some foreign country and have to face what it really meant to fight a Global War on Terrorism. Many of the guys with me had families at home. Some had wives, some had kids, some just had girlfriends and close friends who would pray for us and send us letters while we all were away at training.

As an infantry soldier, I knew I had to be efficient in my job, whether it meant dragging my buddies through the dirt, or patching them up after a gunshot wound. My job was simple. We would be the first to go in and take down the bad guys. I trained like I was planning on living. I was still in basic training on routine schedule, and I trained tactically in a disciplined manner. We focused a lot on discipline and the basic techniques of survival. There were things like land navigation, reading maps, shooting azimuths, and being aware of your surroundings. These were the most important topics covered while in training. I paid much attention to every detail. As long as I was aware of what was going on, I would be okay. That was what the drills taught me. I could never allow myself to get too distracted nor get too comfortable within an area. I learned a good lesson for life: nothing is permanent.

Before I knew it I was putting on a clean uniform and walking down the parade field to graduate. On May 23, 2008, I graduated basic training as an infantry soldier with the United States Army. I trained hard and kept my composure to the best of my ability to the very end.

The next step was to enter the U.S. Army and report to a unit. I left Fort Benning on that same day and flew home for two weeks of relaxation. While home I had the thought at the back of my head that I couldn't get too comfy. I had to stay focused and on track. I reported to Fort Hood, Texas, on June 5, 2008, to the 1st Cavalry, and I was more scared than when I originally entered basic training. I knew that there were going to be a lot of guys that had more rank on their chests and an immense amount of higher authority and experience than me.

It made me nervous being around my new platoon. Here were new men I needed to get to know and get along with whether I wanted to or not. If I were to deploy, I would leave with them, and them only. A little time passed, and I began to get comfortable. I was comforted by most of the new crew and other guys in my unit. The nickname I was given was "Cherry," the new kid on the mortar squad with the most accuracy and talent. What got to the men that were in charge was that Cherry had a bad mouth that included a little spicy New York attitude. It wasn't that I wanted to disrespect the non-commissioned officers above me, but that I knew, even though I was lower rank, that I had the right to rebuttal regarding anything I felt wasn't fair. Either it was that, or something about my smart sarcastic facial gestures… I had the mouth to get me both in and out of trouble.

Having been raised amidst the diversity of Brooklyn and taught that everyone was equal, I did not think that anyone should have to suffer or be put down because of race or heritage. In the army you need to build very thick skin to be able to deal with the jokes and remarks made against you. Even though things said were bound to hurt my feelings, I needed to pull through it and keep moving and working hard, all while keeping a smirk on my face. No smiling, mostly smirking, because it got to them more than to me. They knew I had something in me that made me stand out more than the rest. It all fell back on how I was raised. The rookie on the squad had more attitude and enthusiasm than guys who had been there for years. After a while, I earned my rank. Soon enough my chest wasn't empty any more.

Over time Fort Hood felt like home. The bond and the trust we built there was something that could not be broken nor taken from any of us. We were always training physically, never stopping, never giving up. We were products of military training, and we were being trained to kill. We were the best at what we did, and sometimes we even had to show the top-dog officers how we could perform under pressure, because they and the squad leaders needed the most efficient men to perform the jobs. Some would put in the physical effort to show us techniques; others would stand back and verbally describe how an action was supposed to be performed.

I began to mature and to understand the bigger picture. I will tell you that modern army technique turns a regular individual from a civilian into a sophisticated soldier. I not only obtained a ton of important information on weapon systems, but I also developed "military bearing." Military bearing means a soldier behaves with a certain decorum and discipline. He adheres to the utmost levels of honor, duty, and professionalism in whatever he does. It is most important when in uniform.

Being with the 1st Squadron 7th Cavalry Regiment gave me the feeling of motivation and honor. I was part of the Cavalry that landed in Japan with MacArthur. They had fought some of the bloodiest battles in World War II, and many were massacred in the push over the hills against the Japanese. I didn't really look into all the history, so you must be asking how many units pushed over the hills? Well if you're interested, I'm sure you can Google it. The point is that I was honored to be with the 1st Squadron 7th Cavalry Regiment. It graduated me from being a young kid into a young man.

I came home after basic and everything for me was so different. How was it different, you may ask? I'll tell you. For one thing, I noticed that too many people abuse life and fail to appreciate it, fail to see all that it has to give. There are things like good health, success, wealth, and simple possessions that I will never again take for granted. The simple freedom of hanging your own choice of personal stuff is what got to me most, because when I first entered basic, I was stripped of simple things like body wash and boxers. Everyone had to be in sync. We all had the same underwear. We all had the same bars of soap. We all had the same mentality. We hated it, but once again, I will emphasize, it helped remind us that we were all on the same team fighting for the same cause.

Train, and then train some more, and later finish up with some more training. That is what we were doing after graduation from basic. Deployment was getting closer and closer. I could feel it. I suspected that we were in the field even on weekends, and barely had any days off only because the orders had either come down for deployment, or they were on their way soon. Someone in the higher end of my chain of command knew something that we didn't. We would find out soon enough. As soldiers, we were ready for the fight no matter the situation. We were being worked so hard that as the time came near to head out to the transport "box," many worried that they weren't spending enough time with their kids or their wives. We all sensed that we would leave soon and step foot on some third-world country's soil. We would all go, and we were all prepared. It was only fate that would decide who would make it home in one piece, and who would come home in an 8'x11' box with a flag draped over it. The scary thought was that no one had a clue. We all had anticipated this day for almost eight months.

The time came for us to stand in formation and hear orders read aloud. The 1st Cavalry Division was commanded to take control and oversee all operation in a small region of the south Baghdad province. It dawned on me that I was meant for this, and I was born to fight. I had fear, yet I also had the ambition to do as I was told, and to do as my instincts as a human being told me to do. I saw firsthand how many of my fellow soldiers were fathers leaving behind children who really didn't yet know how to process what daddy was going to do for his country. It was not thoughts of dying a war hero and being greatly honored for it, but it was just the simple cries of "Daddy, come back!" that sent my mind racing.

On February 3, 2009, I dropped my bags off to be collected. I was leaving Fort Hood to complete a mission. It hit me. I became anxious and nervous and emotional and happy and scared and a whole lot of other feelings when I got on the bus to head to the airfield. Not so fortunate for me was the fact that I was alone as I boarded the bus. Many of the others had family members there for support, but my parents couldn't make it out. New York was too far, and the trip would have cost mom her job, and dad just didn't have the personal days to take off. I was always very headstrong and definitely understood why they could not make it out. I kept telling myself that if they had come to Fort Hood to show support before I left, it would have been too emotional for me. I would not have been able to handle it.

So we headed to the airfield at the regional airport in Killeen, Texas. From Killeen we took a commercial flight to Atlanta International Airport. After spending a long holdover in Atlanta, we flew to Maine. When we got to Maine, we transferred to a 757 passenger-carrier from American Airlines to Germany. We were told that the flight would take around 14 hours, weather permitting. This is when I became overwhelmed with emotion and fright. I got on the plane and right away started asking questions. The regular "who, what, when, where, and why" came into play. I needed the comfort and reassurance that we as a team would all be okay. I cared too much for my men, and I definitely treasured my own life, and I figured that I was too young to die at war at the age of 19. The long flight was over before I knew it. I played some video games, did some crossword puzzles, and had some deep conversations with some great guys who sat beside me. I just never knew what to expect next. And then after being in the Frankfurt airport for about eight hours, the real business began to take place. We heard a loud, "All right men, first flight out will be… long pause… and then I heard my name, and lo and behold ANGERT was one of the men going. So, with the other soldiers, I went by bus straight to the landing strip. As the bus pulled up to the plane, I thought, "Oh man, this is it; this is where I begin to give all or nothing. Grab a hold of yourself Sam, everything will be fine. If shit hits the fan, believe me, your training will kick in, and you will do as you were taught to do."

And so the journey from Germany to Kuwait began in a full battle rattle (geared up) on a passenger-carrier Air Force jumbo jet. We later landed in

Sam with captured enemy weapons stash

Kuwait in Ali al Salim and again waited some hours thereafter were taken to Camp Beuring. For those of you who don't know Chinook's are known to be one of the military's fastest helicopters because they have dual propellers. We got on the "bird" and flew to Baghdad International Air Port. It was another 36 hours before we began our first roadside commute in our M1151 armored Humvee. And First Cavalry brigade assumed command on a joint-security station (JSS) in Istiqlal in the south Baghdad province of Iraq–the place I like to call my second home, and place of second birth.

When we got there it didn't seem all too bad in the beginning, so I breathed a huge sigh of relief. The pods where we were staying were almost like little trailers, but each one held three double bunks in it, which meant that a room 8' wide and 20' long had to fit six grown men in it. The biggest issue wasn't going to be the tight space. The biggest issue was going to be how to get along and make sure everything was equal in the space. After a while, everyone's stuff was settled in, and people made their own private area, and the room became home.

While being there and working off the JSS, we would conduct patrols and continue our tour, completing one mission after another. To me, everything we did was important and would help to put an end to the war on terror. We were there for military support and to help the locals–whether it was by meeting with the elders in the small town or by holding large meetings with all the sheiks and leaders in the community. It came down to being there for fellow-soldiers and for the locals as well. Comforting the locals and making sure they felt that they could trust us was a key factor.

We soldiers played a huge role in creating some sort of local governance. We wanted them to feel free to argue and fight about certain things. We then helped the issues get settled after a long discussion. Our focus while we were out among locals was to ensure safety and help build their areas for living, for irrigation, and even for farming. My commander had pledged our support on agriculture. If, and only if, we had to go and take down the bad guys—and most cases occurred because they were causing a disturbance— we would do so as well.

The town there was very little and very tight. The roads were tight, and the wiring was tight because the locals out there had to do it all on their own. They didn't have a Verizon cable guy at the door to fix the phone line. Nor did they have a Direct TV guy to come and fix the Dish. (Although I must say, I did see a lot of dishes on many of the houses out there. God only knows what they were watching.)

Anytime we were on patrol, if I wasn't in the truck itself, either on the gun turret or as the driver, I was patrolling on foot. When I had the pleasure of walking on the ground, I had an awesome opportunity to experience Iraq's heat. The heat could be strong at times that it could make my uniform almost crack. From all the sweat and dry heat beating down on us, we sometimes wouldn't hydrate properly. The combination of energy drinks plus nicotine added to a dehydrated condition and the physical strain could–and would at times–cause heat stroke and fry a soldier's brain. I needed to always be one step ahead of everyone else. That is how I looked at it, because if I didn't, then I would be one of the guys falling out and being placed on the "list." Being on the "shithead list" wouldn't be good, and it definitely wouldn't help me get a promotion. On the other hand, if

I kept myself in check and never needed anyone else to pick it up for me, then I would be okay.

I always thought to myself it was just a game, so to speak. That my time in the military wasn't going to be permanent. Even if I did like the whole 20-year tour of duty, at some point in my mid-40s, I would still have a long life ahead of me. I knew at some future point all the hard work and miserable moments would all be over. We attended a lot of meetings because my commanding staff was focused upon improving security checkpoints and making sure that the police and emergency response unit worked well with us, and they could possibly pick up on our tactics. We performed many missions that involved pulling simple security for our higher ranked officers on the ground. If we had the time to train the Iraqi police or Iraqi army, we did that, too. Officers take precedence in the field. They are more likely targets in a combat zone because Taliban operatives think if they take out our military leadership, the remaining soldiers won't be able to function tactically. The surprise to all is that the officers aren't always as critical to proper functioning as are the lower ranked men! (Ha ha ha).

My deployment was surely going smoothly, and we continued patrolling the outskirts of the south Baghdad province to ensure safety and peace.

I think there comes a point where a Mideast man perceives that his land has been taken over by rebels. And as he envisions this picture in his head, aggression builds in his mind, so he chooses to take it out on the troops. I think the American people here at home don't understand what this war looks like from the Iraqi side. Imagine for a minute what it would be like if we all were sitting on our porches one night, and a convoy of trucks pulled up with soldiers aboard, and dozens of fully armored soldiers jumped out onto our streets carrying loaded weapons. We would be somewhat frightened, don't you think? The reaction here in the United States would be much more severe than the reaction we experienced in Iraq.

The people there weren't as aggressive in the beginning because there is so much unoccupied space remaining in the country. At the same time, there is no established government in Iraq, and no one cares enough to hang up "No Trespassing" signs, so a lot of the free land out there is a "no-man's land." After troops have been in Iraq for a while, interactions can fluctuate between good and better, but they also can plummet from bad to worse. The locals begin to like us. They get used to our presence and accept us for always helping. (As Yogi Berra was fond of saying, "The night ain't over 'til the fat lady sings.") But then after we have been in the country a long time, the population begins to get mad and upset with us. They feel that we have been there too long, and they claim that their cries for help go unanswered, with no one attending to the locals' needs. Envy sets in when things are about to get hectic.

It was just like any other day when I was patrolling the same main supply route. We were supposed to begin the patrol in route to a meeting to discuss plans for a future local project. That morning seemed like a regular day to me, as it did to the rest of my men. You never know what the endless possible outcomes of war truly are until it is over. In a worst-case scenario, you shoot first, ask questions later. To fail the objective at hand was never an option. I always knew that I would have someone—if not all of the guys—beside me for both moral and physical support. As long as there was a voice screaming or another rifle firing, I was on my feet and ready. "Trust me."

On August 23, 2009, a Sunday morning in the south Baghdad province of Iraq, a convoy from the 1st Squadron 7th Cavalry Regiment was hit with a newly improved and devastating powerful explosive called an improvised

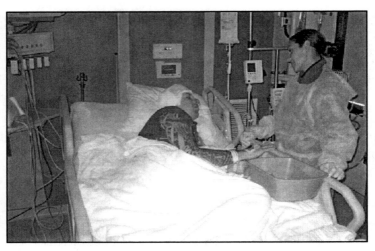

Sam recovering after his fifth and final open-brain surgery

explosive device (IED). The blast demobilized our first vehicle, while the other two trucks hundreds of meters behind watched in shock and awe. The explosion from the IED hurt a few people including me. The gunner in my vehicle got hit in his left femoral artery. The two men in the back, who would have been dismounts that day, walked out with minor concussions and nothing more than a headache. My lieutenant, 2nd Lieutenant Joseph Fortin, was killed instantly. And everything that went into him came right through into the right side of my face. At the split second when all of this happened, I blacked out.

I woke up about fifteen days later. I shifted in and out of consciousness thanks to a medically induced coma. On September 10, 2009, I woke up to a room full of people. I did not know who they were or where I was. My mind raced with questions: What happened? Where did all of you come from? Where am I? How did you all get here? This is so far from Iraq. Mom, what are you doing here? It's so far from home. Who brought you here? I was utterly disoriented and unaware of my surroundings. My poor brain did not know how to process all this at once. Little by little, my memory returned and I recalled what had happened to me. I became more aware of myself. I found myself being spoon-fed Jell-O by my mother and knew that I desperately needed to get out of my miserable state of mind and body. But how?

It was time for a come-to-God talk with myself. I decided that I would not allow anything or anyone to hold me back from my new mission—getting better. I wouldn't allow people to look at me with pity because I was severely hurt. I wouldn't simply give up on myself because as soon as I did that, settle for failure, others around me would feel the same way. I looked at my traumatic injury this way:

> "My success will depend upon how I stabilize my mind. It will depend upon how I look at things and how I deal with the obstacles that I will come across. I was born a New Yorker with a big mouth, a determined personality, and a resilient spirit that will soldier me through."

I ended up alive. The blast from the IED had caused a traumatic brain injury and multiple other injuries. A piece of shrapnel lodged about an inch below my right eye. Because of the immediate danger to my eye, surgery to remove the metal fragment was done in Iraq. I also had surgery to reconstruct my right cheekbone, which was shattered from the shrapnel.

God has been good, and He has given me another mission beyond the army. I need to recover and discover what it is. There are only so much the physicians and the surgeons in trauma and rehab teams can do for me. They played a major role in my physical recovery—five open-brain surgeries and three facial reconstructions among many other procedures—but in the long run, for me, survival is all about the way that I value and embrace my new life. So that is what I did and continue to do, to the fullest. After I got through several stages of misery and sadness, I began to see my injury as a positive event. I accepted it, and I understood from that moment on that there was about to be a second birth of a new Sam Angert.

The new Sam Angert is who I am now, and who I am going to be until the day I die. I will not let my injury define me as a person, because truly, even though you can tell that my face has been hurt by war, that injury does not make me who I really am. I survived and recovered from traumatic injury by digging deep inside myself and pulling out the courage and resilience that I was known for long before my time in Iraq. I knew it wasn't going to be easy, and recovery would take some time, but I had both the time and energy I needed to rebuild my life. I take one day at a time and still do that today. I managed carefully my psychological energy and trained myself to be more adaptable and to have more stamina. By just taking it day by day, I know that eventually the day will come when I will look in the mirror and be content with my new face and my new capabilities.

There isn't much else I can say except that I took my chances. I dedicated my young adult life to the military and shed blood for the flag that I wore on my right shoulder. I did it freely and today, I stay determined to complete my personal missions, no matter what.

I am the new Samuel Michael Angert. I wasn't expected to survive; yet I walked away from traumatic injury almost three years later.

Sam with Purple Heart

This story is dedicated to Second Lieutenant Joseph Fortin and to my mother, Polina Drabkin. Mom is an amazing woman and the strongest person I have known in my life. I am blessed to have her. I love you mom. You're the best!

I extend a loving thank you to all those who supported me. I am a remarkable success story because of your support. I will continue to live my life to the fullest with a grateful head on my shoulder and a good story to tell.

Steve's Story

I n the winter of 1985, in a small city in rural Southern Illinois, I Steven Baskis took my first breath and set eyes on my loving parents and the world. Clearly, I don't remember any of it, yet when I find myself pondering that particular experience, I can't help but relate it to an equally transitional date that occurred in my later life.

That traumatic day was May 13, 2008, when an explosion in the Middle East took away my sight while I was serving with the U.S. Army. Other soldiers, Marines, airmen, and sailors may describe their survival after near-death combat experiences as a rebirth, a second chance at life, or the beginning of a new normal, but for me, it was the beginning of a life in darkness, a life of permanent blindness.

My story begins with another much earlier explosion. During my childhood, my father often reminisced about how happy I was as a baby. He liked to retell how I often made very jolly and incongruous responses to the evening news on television, specifically, the news broadcast of the

Challenger shuttle explosion. He would describe how I bounced, laughed, and smiled whenever the tragic disaster was rebroadcast. I was a baby, of course, so I could not understand the sudden loss of life that was captured on that dramatic video. Now, 26 years later, I have a much deeper understanding of what happened. Normalcy ended in a single explosion.

Between 1985 and 2004, I moved with my family to several states in the Northeast, Midwest, and Southwest. This was because my father traveled quite a bit for his business, and our family always tagged along behind. All of this moving and traveling during my childhood allowed me to gain knowledge of our country's regional histories and cultures. I felt extremely fortunate to have so many insightful experiences at a young age as a result of all my family's relocations. Adjusting and adapting to new situations became one of my strong personal qualities, and I relied on this talent when it was time to attend new schools, make new friends, or explore new neighborhoods.

My two younger brothers would probably agree with me when I say that we were not indulged with a lot of toys and possessions and did not grow up with fancy things, but we were happy. We were content with our two arms and legs, our imaginations, and our sense of exploration. My brothers and I spent many days running along a winding creek that lay deep in a forest behind our home in Carbondale, Illinois. We climbed trees and played soldier games. Our father explained that his three little boys would probably end up destroying fancy things anyway. So my brothers and I simply enjoyed the great outdoors and our family travels.

By the time I was 12 years old, we moved to a small town near Sedona, Arizona. There we explored all the red rock we could find by hiking, mountain biking, climbing the red rock mesas, and exploring the desert. I remember pulling cactus needles out of my bike's tires every day that I went for a ride.

The high elevation and dry desert climate of Arizona was not our home for very long, though, because we moved again. This time, my dad moved us all the way across the country to New York. As the year 2000 approached, my brothers and I found ourselves exploring the urban jungle of Manhattan. Big city living was different, but we made great friends once again, and we slowly adapted to fast-paced city life.

Military life was the norm for my family and probably one of the reasons for our nomadic lifestyle. Many of my extended family members had served our country with honor and pride. My aunt, uncle, grandfather and father all served or worked with the Air Force, Army, or Navy. I believe their service to our country and their experiences, which they shared with me, influenced my decision to enlist. I remember sitting with my grandfather and listening to his stories of his travels to Europe and North Africa during World War II. Every time he told me something new, I would look into the history of the campaign or battle. All of these interactions with war stories and military service fueled my desire for more adventures and travel.

Long Island, New York was probably one of my favorite places among the many spots my family called home. While all Americans will forever remember their pain at witnessing that horrible day of September 11, 2001, it was even more painful for those of us who lived nearby. For me, the images of aircrafts slamming into the twin towers, people leaping to their death, and the buildings crashing to the city streets below, will forever be seared into my psyche. I did not live very far from the city and throughout that day, I could hear ambulances, fire engines, and emergency vehicles racing with sirens blaring towards the smoldering destruction that lay on Manhattan Island. But it wasn't until the very next day, when I arrived at school, that the real hard truth hit home. People had lost their lives. Friends and classmates were absent from school because a family member or friend had not made it home…and sadly some would never make it home. September 11 changed my life, my family's life, and the world forever. And, although I was only age 16, joining the military was back on my mind.

I approached a Marine recruiter when I was 17 years old. I was very interested in what military occupations were available. In my mind, I understood what was at stake. There was a war occurring 9,000 miles away, and our country was involved. Men and women were dying and suffering traumatic injuries. It was no secret to me that, if I joined the military, I might come home a different person, or not come home at all. Since the military had always been part of my family's legacy, I turned to my family and friends for questions and used the Internet and books to do additional research. I watched the news and tried to mentally grasp the history that was unfolding right before my eyes. I knew that for me to be part of the fight, I needed to better understand our government, the military, and the distant foreign countries.

Although I met with a Marine recruiter initially, I waited a few years before enlisting into the U.S. Army to be trained as an Infantryman. When I finally did enlist, I was driven to succeed. I viewed joining and serving in the U.S. Army as a way to build a foundation, a stepping stone towards pursuing higher education and a professional career. If I decided to stay in, that would be great. If I decided to leave the Army after my contract ended, that would be fine too. I was truly looking at making the Army a long career, though, one that I knew would be filled with trials and tribulations, but a career that I could look back upon and feel that my life had true meaning.

To become a professional soldier, that was what I wanted more than anything. In the Army, there are many units and divisions, but there is one community that captured my attention, the special operations community. Volunteering initially for Infantry Training was important because if I later decided to make Army my career, I could volunteer for Special Forces Assessment and Selection (SFAS). I reasoned that starting as an Infantryman or Rifleman would build the mental and physical foundation required for me to pursue Special Forces. I had my dreams, and I had my goals. All that remained to be done was to sign the enlistment papers and ship off to basic training.

I left for Fort Benning, Georgia, home of the U.S. Army's infantry for basic and advanced training in January of 2007. The first week or so at Fort Benning, I learned an important lesson: hurry up and wait. Delays occurred so often that I thought standing was all that I was going to do in the Army from that point forward. Finally we moved into our training barracks where we met our drill sergeants.

I will never forget my first day of training. It was hilarious. The drill sergeants met us at the bottom of a hill. They jumped aboard our bus and screamed, "Get the hell off my bus." We had packed our gear into big duffle bags and placed them above our heads on the bus. The kid in front of me got clobbered in the head when a duffle fell as the bus came to a stop. Everyone jumped off the bus and started up the hill with the bags on their shoulders. I was in a dead sprint. I remember to this day that the drill sergeants were

Steve joining the Army

picking off all the slow runners and forcing them to do all kinds of additional exercises on our flanks.

Basic training continued in this chaotic state until the last day of training in May of 2007. The training was more psychologically intense than anything else. I had a great time and did what I was ordered to do. It was simple as that. What was not so simple, in the beginning, was trying to get our 30-man platoon to work together as a team. I tried to explain to the recruits, whether we do things perfectly or not was not the issue. The drill sergeants were going to find something wrong and drill us into the ground anyway, so we just needed to do our best and work together. My drill sergeants thought I showed some leadership skills during training, so during our graduation ceremony, I was awarded a meritorious promotion. I was really just trying to get through by helping the individuals that I thought were having the most trouble. It helped me to focus and successfully graduate from infantry training.

I was assigned to the 4th Infantry Division 4th Brigade at Fort Hood, Texas, in the summer of 2007. The division has a proud history as some 4th Infantry Division units actually crossed the beaches of Normandy, France, during World War II, and they fought hard during the Vietnam War. I was proud of my accomplishments up until then, and I wanted to move into an infantry line unit as soon as possible, so I could gain more experience and skills.

I learned my second lesson as soon as I arrived at Fort Hood: The army will put you where they need people, not necessarily where you want to go. My first day at Fort Hood was not so great. A Sergeant First Class thought I would better serve in his office. I guess he liked my discipline and ability to communicate respectfully to higher enlisted and officer soldiers. I feared that I was going to be an infantryman on paper, and that was disappointing to me because I did not want to work in an office. I told myself to go with the flow, and my time would come later to pursue my specific goals. I vowed to drive on and do my best.

One day I overheard some officers and sergeants talking about a special unit that was going to be assembled. The unit would be built around a platoon of four squads, each squad consisting of approximately 13 men who would be responsible for protecting an individual. The platoon was a Personal Security Detachment for the 4th Infantry Division Commanders. The Command had three Generals and a Division Command Sergeant Major. When I learned that this assignment was open to anyone, I volunteered on the spot. I knew it would get me out of the office, into more training, and into the fight. That was what I wanted and what I was trained to do.

I realized quickly that this would be a very different mission from what ordinary infantryman usually do. The primary role of a personal security specialist or bodyguard is to protect an individual and not to engage and fight the enemy. I would be trained in advance operations, protective driving and shooting, how to interact and work with a "principal," (the person being protected) and much, much more. My favorite part of the training was motorcade and convoy tactical formation, driving, and transition drills with weapons. Each squad trained every day of every week up until our deployment, rehearsing and practicing our operating procedures and tactics.

I will never forget the day I left for the Middle East. A single aircraft stood on the tarmac for our platoon, which would be the first one into Iraq before the whole 4th Infantry Division arrived. The sky was grey and overcast. A lonely army band positioned near the stairs to the plane was playing a patriotic tune in the wind and rain. I stared at my surroundings and into the eyes of the band members as I walked past them onto the plane. It was a gloomy and depressing departure from the United States. I looked outside the airplane window, not knowing that this would be the last time my eyes would clearly see American soil. Our 16-month deployment had begun.

Delta Company, 1st Platoon, the group with whom I was attached, finally arrived in Baghdad, Iraq in late 2007. We had flown in on a C-17 Globe Master into Baghdad International Airport from Kuwait. A Sergeant Major greeted us near the aircraft and shuttled us off to where we would live for the next 16 months. I remember seeing the first pair of UH-60 Black-hawk helicopters fly over me low and fast as I shuffled to the vehicle.

The environment around me seemed very alien. I saw tan desert and blue sky everywhere I looked. In some areas where there was running water, I noticed lush green vegetation growing, and in others, there was just hard rock and barren sand with no signs of life. The homes and buildings were also desert tan. They seemed to spring from the ground, as if they had grown from the earth beneath them. Wild dogs seemed to be roaming everywhere in small packs, scavenging for food and whatever they could find along the garbage-filled city streets.

Baghdad, was a city filled with markets, buildings and thousands of windows and doors. It was extremely difficult to scan and observe every nook and cranny for enemies while on a mission. The atmosphere above us felt electric and dangerous, since the enemy was known for lobbing artil-lery and rockets onto our fortified bases and locations. The veteran soldiers explained to us that a siren would blare to alert of us of an enemy attack. It would then be our job to find cover if the artillery was landing on our position. I experienced a number of artillery and rocket barrages while on the ground in Iraq. Some occurred while we were walking on base, some while we were traveling in, and others while we were visiting small outposts. Sniper fire and suicide bombers were always on my mind as well, especially when we were out on a mission or patrol.

On May 13, 2008, my squad was assigned a mission. The mission handed down to us involved traveling to a specific destination North of Baghdad. We were to escort and protect the Brigadier General and safely drop him off at a secure location. The day started out fairly normal. At first there was not going to be a mission, but that changed around noon when we were informed of this operation. I ate lunch in my humvee and took the position of driver for the lead vehicle. All the weapons, ammunition and medical gear had been checked. My short-barreled, adjustable butt-stock M249 sat next to me locked and loaded. The 13-plus soldiers in my squad sat ready in our idling up-armored vehicles, patiently waiting for the General to exit the headquarters building, so we could embark on our long drive to our objective.

The first half of the mission went very well. We encountered no enemy fire or roadside bombs. We pulled into the secure fortified base, where our General was going to disembark and meet a sister unit who would help him complete his assigned work. At this point it was decided that part of the team would stay with the General, and the other would return to our home base. I was part of the team that would return to home base.

Again my squad prepared to make the journey back through Baghdad to our forward operating base. We locked and loaded our weapons, conducted a

Steve enjoying a little down time outside the Green Zone in Central Bagdad

radio check, and headed southbound back into the city. I drove the armored vehicle down a pot-marked and severely deteriorating road, scanning left to right in front of the vehicles hood. I was looking for any sign of roadside bombs or enemies. We past crumbling bridges, old beat-up Russian tanks, and small cars, but no shots or explosions came.

Almost half way back to our home base, our convoy approached a traffic circle on the northern edge of Baghdad. I pushed the armored vehicle through the intersection and out the other side, and that was when the explosion happened. It came so hard and fast that I don't even remember it. The team and vehicle behind ours later explained that an explosive device detonated off to our right side and that the explosion propelled a piece of metal at the right passenger door. Victor, my team leader, was sitting on the side where the blast hit our armored vehicle.

Fire, sand, rock and shrapnel tore through the interior cabin and into Victor.

Victor, I believe, absorbed most of the blast, because of where he was seated, protecting me from deadly flames and flying debris. Small pieces of shrapnel hit me in my head, neck, arms, and legs. I was knocked unconscious and started to bleed all over.

My team reacted to the situation and pulled Victor and me from the damaged vehicle as fast as they could. A number of days later, I awoke groggy and disoriented in a military hospital in Washington, D.C. Victor had suffered a traumatic and severe injury and died there on the road that evening. Our medic, along with two other individuals, rushed to help me. I was losing a lot of blood and needed to be evacuated from the area. A helicopter was called in to transport me to a field hospital, so a surgeon could stop the arterial bleeding and address the other injuries that I sustained.

I awoke groggy and disoriented in a military hospital in Washington, D.C. a number of days later. I felt like I was dreaming when I first awoke. It took my brothers a good while to help orient me to where I was and why I was there. Slowly the heavy dosages of medicine wore off, and I regained the ability to think clearly. The whole experience still seemed like a horrible nightmare to me. One that I could not comprehend. I had been in a combat zone a few days ago, half a world away from the hospital bed where I now lay.

Doctors and nurses came to visit me off and on during those few first days to see how I was doing. One of the head physicians explained that my eyes were damaged so badly that he was unsure whether or not I would ever see again. I went in for a surgery, hoping that I would recover some sort of light perception, but I understood deep down that I probably would never see the world as I did before my injury.

My mind was lost in memories of sight and life before May 13th and of a future in darkness. I asked myself how was I going too live this way? I made it out of the hospital bed a week-and-a-half after getting to Walter Reed. My legs had sustained injuries, but they were not as severe or debilitating as my head injuries. I said to myself, if I can't see, I better be able to walk and run. I started working with my physical therapist and occupational therapist. They had me doing all kinds of exercises and stretches. My hands were both injured in the blast, so it was very hard to feed myself early on. My family helped me eat. My left arm had serious blood vessel and nerve damage, and I had lost all sensation and fine motor control. In my mind this injury, on top of being blind, made me feel very weak and helpless at times.

Every night that I lay in bed at that hospital, I thought of my goals, dreams, and promises made before joining the military and shipping off to war. I remembered how important it was to me to have a strong mind and body, so I could handle the stress and rigors of war. I thought about my dream to become a Green Beret, a seasoned, professional soldier. Most importantly, I thought about the promise I made to myself and my family, to never give up and to always try my best, if not my hardest, to live a great life.

One day a person from an organization named The Blinded Veterans Association came to visit me at the hospital. I had probably only been at the hospital for two or three weeks at that point, and I was healing and recovering fast. The man from the Association explained to me that the next step to recovering was to attend a blind rehabilitation center and learn the necessary skills and techniques to live life independently. Instantly, I had a new goal and some sort of direction. I told him, that's exactly where I want to go. Plus, it was my ticket out of the hospital and the road to full recovery.

Walter Reed discharged me a month and a half after losing my vision, so I could attend blind rehabilitation at Hines Veterans Administration

Steve receiving the Purple Heart

Hospital near Chicago, Illinois. I was medically evacuated and flown by
C1-30 from the Washington D.C. area to Chicago.

When I arrived in Chicago, I was nervous, anxious, and excited about
starting blind rehab training, but I knew deep down that it was extremely
important for me too begin this process early. A blind rehabilitation specialist at the hospital had volunteered to be my orientation and mobility
instructor. This person is responsible for teaching a blind individual how
to navigate streets and hallways independently. The amazing thing was that
this lady who volunteered to help me had a connection to my family and
to one of the towns where I had lived. She had grown up in a house that
was directly across the pond from my cousins' home in Central Illinois. Her
father was a dentist who had treated my younger brothers. This wild coin-
cidence and connection made me think about my life and how small the
world can be. I was going to work with a person whom I never met, but who
had grown up in one of my many hometowns.

Orientation and mobility training was not easy. I had to learn how to
travel with a long white cane, move down busy sidewalks and hallways,
and navigate in unfamiliar places. It was the last thing I wanted to do. I felt
like a baby, a kid, a person who had to learn how to walk all over again. The
rehab specialists would have me navigate routes by using my other senses,

and this was extremely slow and frustrating in the beginning. A simple walk from the blind center to the hospital cafeteria became daunting and tedious. Water fountains, vending machines, air conditioning units, and strange noises in specific places, helped me navigate the black labyrinth, which was how the massive hospital complex appeared to me.

I learned very quickly that I needed to be patient. I needed to relax and understand how to use my other senses to my advantage. If I could not master these skills and techniques, mine would be a long life of just sitting home on a couch doing absolutely nothing and being afraid of the world.

Next I graduated to outdoor mobility, which involved navigating residential and commercial streets. Navigating outdoors when you are blind can be very unsettling and nerve-racking, especially when you have heavy motor vehicles barreling down roads a few feet from where you are walking. I kept fearing being hit by a distracted driver or motorist when I was practicing crossing intersections. Slamming my cane down on the sidewalk in frustration became the norm.

I was fed up with being blind and helpless. Sometimes I just wanted to give up. I thought about my buddy Victor and other guys I had met who had it far worse than me. Instantly, I stopped feeling sorry for myself. I thought back to my military training and realized that I was trained to be resilient. I was trained to adapt and evolve.

A soldier, Marine, airman or sailor lives a very different life, especially on the battlefield. It is generally a challenging and rigorous lifestyle. Well, I had asked for this kind of life. I had volunteered for military service with high hopes of becoming an intelligent, well-trained warrior who could live a normal life and flip a switch when the bullets came whizzing. My blindness was going to be a lifelong challenge, but it would never be as difficult as war and the hardships that I had already faced on the battlefield. I needed to re-evaluate my situation and what I wanted from life moving forward. I needed to adapt and try my hardest to find a way to live again.

All through out my training and recovery my family and friends visited me, encouraging me and supporting me through the hard times. I spent time talking to my brothers and my mother and father about what was next, and about what I could do when I was finished with rehabilitation. I decided that I was going to try and regain my physical health and fitness, since I had lost a significant amount of weight and muscle. Cycling seemed like the best option at the time and a great way to build my leg strength, so I spun away.

About halfway through my blind rehabilitation, I met a wonderful and amazing person who changed my life once again. Her name is Sarah. She came into my life when I least expected it. At the time, I felt that I was different, someone who was a burden and a problem. I never dreamed that I would find a loving and caring person who would look past my vision loss and treat me like a normal human being. Sarah instilled in me much hope and a drive, a motivating force, to accomplish the goals that meant the most to me. Each and every day my spirits and confidence soared, and I progressed through my blind rehabilitation training, setting goals and dreaming of a future with Sarah at my side.

Five months past in a flash, and the doctors decided to discharge me from the hospital. I moved into an apartment near the hospital and prepared to plan for my future. One day a representative from the United States Association of Blind Athletes gave a presentation to the hospital staff about rehabilitation through sports, recreation, and physical fitness. I caught word of the presentation and received some information about a cycling camp that U.S. Paralympics organizes. I wanted to give tandem cycling a chance (a bike designed for two people). I entered a road-race and time-trial, and my partner and I pushed our tandem cycle to over 40 miles per hour. It was truly a great time. I fell in love with tandem cycling, and I continue to ride, train, and compete in this sport throughout the year.

I remain involved with sports and recreation. In late 2010, I was invited to be part of a team of injured veterans whose goal was to summit a 20,000-foot mountain in the Himalayas. The entire climb was filmed and documented and at the time of this writing premiered in Boulder, Colorado. *High Ground,* the name of the film, tells the personal story of eleven veterans and their fight to push through barriers and overcome adversity.

The past four years have been a wild and crazy ride. I've done my best to hold on to my values and beliefs, and I believe they have protected me from drifting even further into darkness and depression. The experiences of my childhood and life in the military have given me the ability to think through my problems, frustrations, and weaknesses. The people in my life—my caring family, great friends and organizations and the country in general—have always been at my side, mentoring and guiding me during hard times. I continue to look ahead to greater and even better things, understanding that bad things do happen to all of us.

Steve and father boating on the Ohio River in 2007

I am Steve Baskis, and I was born to be resilient.

Here is what I have learned from all the adversity that I have faced. No matter what happens, if you think positively, never dwell on the negative, never give up on yourself, and drive as hard and as fast as you can forward, nothing will keep you from building and living a great life.

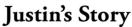

Justin's Story

A lthough I barely remember October 18, 2006, it is a day I will never forget. It is the day that I was shot in the head by an enemy sniper in Iraq, and the day that my life changed forever. However, despite some rough times and dark days, I like where life has taken me and do not regret volunteering for that deployment.

Although my primary military occupation specialty is that of a Judge Advocate, I deployed in 2006 as a Civil Affairs Team Leader. I had served on active duty in the Marine Corps from 1998 to 2004, working almost exclusively in the field of criminal law, both as a prosecutor and as a defense counsel. In 2005, I joined a Reserve unit whose mission was to teach deploying units different aspects of the law of war and rules of engagement. In June 2006, I transferred to the 4th Civil Affairs Group in Washington, D.C., in time for their upcoming fall deployment.

A Captain at the time, I led a team of seven Marines and a Navy Corpsman. Fortunately for me, most of my Marines had already deployed to Iraq before. My non-commissioned officers were rock solid and made my job a lot easier. We trained hard that summer in Washington and at a few nearby bases, determined what each of our responsibilities would be, and started to function well together as a team.

Although our headquarters unit was in Fallujah, our team actually spent very little time there. Not long after we arrived in the country, we were attached to 3rd Battalion, 2nd Marines, a Marine infantry battalion out of Camp Lejeune, North Carolina. They operated out of Camp Habbaniyah, and were pushing westwards towards Ramadi. I remember reporting in to the Battalion Commander, Lieutenant Colonel Todd Desgrosseilliers, and can still picture on the wall outside his office the photographs of the young Marines in the 3rd Battalion who had already been killed by the enemy. Like images from a high school yearbook, these young men were still teenagers, which, for some reason made their deaths even more sad.

As a Civil Affairs Officer, I was expected to develop contracts with the local population to help rebuild the basic infrastructure needed for any city: clean running water, functioning electricity, drivable roads and well-needed schools. Unfortunately, the *Fall of 2006* was an extremely volatile time for the Marine Corps in Iraq, and the insurgency there was at its most powerful level. Convincing the local Iraqis to work with us to rebuild the cities was virtually impossible when they would be visited at night by members of the insurgency with death threats for any indication of cooperation. That being said, I will always look back on the time I spent in Iraq as the highlight of my career—not too many other lawyers get to lead Marines in a combat environment, and I learned a lot about myself, and effective leadership, while I was there.

Because I worked closely with the Battalion Commander, he put me on his "jump team," which was comprised of about a dozen Marines who went out "across the wire" together about four or five times per week. We were on a regular combat patrol that day, and we got to an area where we knew an enemy sniper had already killed a few Marines, but of course that wasn't going to interfere with our mission.

We actually had a reporter with us that day, and he and others have reiterated to me what happened, because I don't remember most of it. Earlier in

Justin (leftmost) and fellow Marines in Iraq in 2006

the day, we had stopped at one of our forward operating bases to check on our Marines, and apparently I noticed that the reporter was kind of standing around, and not continually moving in order to avoid being an easy target for a sniper.

Well, when we got out of the vehicle at our next stop and started walking away from the Humvee, I told the reporter that he needed to move faster or he might get shot. Based on that, he took a big step forward, and a split second later a round came in right where his head had been and hit the wall behind us. The next shot hit me right behind my ear and exited out my mouth, causing catastrophic damage along the way. In fact, the Marines around me thought that I had been killed, and when the Corpsman came running over, they told him, "Don't worry about the Major – he's dead."

But Keiran Grant is an amazing young man, and even though blood was pouring out of my head and over what was left of my face, and even though the sniper was still trying to pick off the Marines, he proceeded to save my life. As shattered and damaged as my face was, Corpsman Grant performed rescue breathing on me, and also did an emergency tracheotomy, so that I wouldn't drown in my own blood. In the face of overwhelming adversity, and with complete disregard for his own life, Keiran performed perfectly. In fact, despite that situation, he had done such a wonderful job on my tracheotomy that my plastic surgeon at the military hospital thought another surgeon had performed it.

After I was shot, my team sprang into action to protect me and to identify the threat. Lieutenant Colonel Desgrosseilliers was then faced with a tough choice–call in an emergency airlift and wait for the helicopter, or drive me to the nearest aid station in an effort to stabilize me. He opted for Lance Corporal Buehler to drive me, and told him to drive as fast as possible. We drove 70 miles per hour to the aid station, and while that is no big deal here at home, in Iraq, we only drove 15 miles per hour wherever we went. At that time, there were so many improvised explosive devices–called IEDs–in the roads that hitting one happened every day. We had learned the hard way that driving faster than 15 miles per hour dramatically increased the chances of the vehicle flipping over upon impact with the IED, and, therefore, it put everyone's lives at risk. However, just like Corpsman Grant had done earlier while saving me, Lance Corporal Buehler put his own life on the line for me, and drove 70 miles per hour to get me to the hospital.

I ultimately arrived at the Naval Hospital at Bethesda, and my life was turned upside down and inside out, but one person held everything together for me from then on. Her name is Dahlia. Now, back then, in 2006, Dahlia and I were not married. In fact, we did not get married until 2008. We had met earlier in 2006 at a Spanish immersion course in Buenos Aires, Argentina. Dahlia was there from California, and I came from Virginia. We were in the same small class, and although I was only there for three weeks, we really hit it off during that short time. We dated that summer back in the States, and then when I deployed to Iraq, Dahlia left to pursue her Ph.D. degree at Cambridge University in England. Contrary to the rules in previous wars, though, Dahlia and I were still able to communicate by email, letters, and packages and by making occasional satellite phone calls.

When I was initially airlifted out of Iraq, they took me to the military hospital in Landstuhl, Germany. Although it was pretty unusual for the service members there to get personal visits, Dahlia was able to get there from England. I was there for four days, and when they sent me on to Bethesda, Dahlia decided to temporarily drop out of her doctoral program to be with me in the hospital (Because of the severity of my injuries, Dahlia was not able to return to Cambridge, but we plan on going there together in five years to resume studies). Never mind that studying at Cambridge was a lifelong dream of hers, or that she didn't know anyone in Maryland or Virginia, or that, at that point in my recovery, the doctors didn't even know if I would survive. When I awoke from my coma, Dahlia was there. And she has been there at my side every day since my traumatic injury. Dahlia has been and remains my inspiration and my "rock."

Despite the extensive damage to my head, I was an in-patient at Bethesda for only five weeks. However, Dahlia spent almost every waking moment of that five weeks in that hospital, even while I was in a coma. We were very fortunate that the parents of one of my best friends lived right down the street from the hospital, and Dahlia was able to stay with them. Somehow, the two of us managed to laugh a lot while I recovered there, although we went through some very trying times.

I could not speak for the first several weeks there, and because my head and neck were so swollen, the doctors could not verify if Corpsman Grant had accidentally cut my vocal cords when he saved my life in Iraq (an accident which would have been understandable under those arduous circumstances). At first, I would only communicate with Dahlia, and did so by tracing out each letter of the word I wanted to say on the palm of her

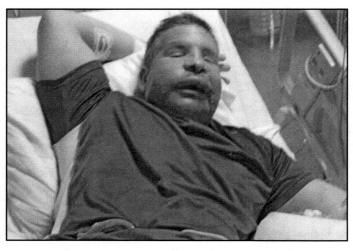

Justin recovering in hospital room in 2008

hand. She can be incredibly patient though, and would translate what I was "saying" for hours at a time. I then progressed to writing out everything I had to say, and got to the point where I could write fast enough to somewhat carry on a conversation with my visitors.

I can still remember when I first started talking again. I was in the Intensive Care Unit (ICU), and heard the nurses talking about me, and of course Dahlia was right there. I looked over at her, and repeated my last name, which I had just heard one of the nurses say. Dahlia did a double-take and ran over. I repeated "Constantine," although it sounded muffled and mumbled because I was missing almost all of my teeth and the end of my tongue. I was heavily sedated. Dahlia started crying immediately, and went to call my parents with the good news.

I spent most of the five weeks in the hospital in my bed, rotating from surgery to surgery and never fully understanding what had happened. My first surgery there lasted 18 hours, and the doctors said that if they waited 12 more hours, my whole face would have caved in on itself. Per the doctors' instructions, Dahlia and my mother taped up get-well cards that I had received on the window and mirror so that I would not be able to see my own reflection. They feared that I would have such a negative reaction upon seeing my new face. I now have a long scar across the top of my head which stretches from ear to ear, where the doctors had to cut open my scalp during that surgery in order to peel down my face to better repair the severe damage caused by one solitary bullet. They also removed the fibula bone from each leg to use in reconstructing my upper and lower jaws. I still cannot see out of my left eye due to scar tissue on my retina, a condition that is not something they can remedy.

Somehow Dahlia and I laughed during these very trying times. We talked about the places we wanted to visit and explore once I recovered. We spent hours glued to marathon sessions of HBO's "The Wire," which someone had generously bought for us. As my legs recovered, we walked very slowly around the hospital, progressing from my first walk just from the bed to the bathroom door, and then later to the nurses' station, and then to a whole lap around that particular wing. There is something to be said for small victories!

Dahlia, Gary Sinise, and Justin in 2008

I also remember walking Dahlia to our car at night when it was time for her to go (oftentimes hours after visiting hours were officially over), and then going back to my room and bed, now so lonely without Dahlia. Even though I knew she needed to go home to get some sleep and good food, I always wished she could stay in my room (which she actually did sometimes even though that meant she slept in a chair or wedged into my tiny bed).

When we left the hospital, Dahlia was still my fulltime caregiver. I was on a feeding tube, and would remain so for several months. Several times a day she would pour my nutritional protein shake into the tube which connected right to my stomach, and we would joke about whether I preferred chocolate or vanilla, as if I could taste them. Dahlia drove us everywhere we needed to go, and I often needed her help walking or with any number of daily living activities. Dahlia put everything in her life on hold for me, and never complained about that. I have seen plenty of relationships with other wounded warriors fall apart due to the incredible stress that the injury placed on that relationship, but in Dahlia's mind it was a no-brainer that she would be there to take care of me.

Although I periodically returned to Bethesda for more surgeries as an outpatient, at some point my plastic surgeon told us that he was leaving for a fellowship at another hospital, and he recommended that I go see the doctors at Johns Hopkins University. That turned out to be the best thing that happened to me. I have received amazing care from Dr. Rodriguez and Dr. Sinada at Hopkins. They are truly experts in what they do. In fact, I have met several other wounded warriors with similar gunshot wounds that have also been patients of Dr. Rodriguez, and we all swear by him. Dahlia and I became intimately familiar with the route between our house in Falls Church, Virginia, and Johns Hopkins University in Baltimore, Maryland. We always looked forward to those trips because they meant I was one step closer to the light at the end of the tunnel.

The night before we had to drive out to Baltimore for a scheduled surgery in 2007, I asked Dahlia if she wanted to see the Marine Corps Iwo Jima Memorial in Arlington. We had planned on going to a Marine Corps Silent Drill Team performance there a few days later, but because I would be in the hospital, we would not be able to attend, yet I still wanted her to see this iconic statue. I arranged to meet Dahlia at the Metro station a few blocks away from the Memorial, and then as the sun set in the distance, we walked the short distance together.

Although we spent almost every waking minute together, I was able, through the surreptitious help of a friend, to buy an engagement ring and have it delivered to our house without Dahlia knowing. And my plan was to propose to Dahlia at the Memorial the night before this next surgery (I was scheduled to be in the hospital close to a week). Well, we got up to the Iwo Jima, and I explained the significance of it to her, and the ring was burning a hole in my pocket.

Unfortunately, this was in the summertime, and the Memorial was one of the monuments that the tourists visited on their evening tours, so every few minutes, just as the people around us would walk off, another bus would pull up and disgorge another loud, pointing group of sightseers. I finally timed it just right, got down on one knee, and asked Dahlia to marry me.

Approximately 18 months later we were married, and we held our ceremony and reception at the Marine Corps Museum outside of the base at Quantico. Most of the men were in their Marine dress uniforms, including me, and Dahlia looked gorgeous in her white dress. And because we had met in Argentina, we chose to dance a tango for our wedding dance. Of course we had to take a series of lessons to learn it, but we pulled it off. In fact, Dahlia changed into a red tango dress for it, and we actually looked like we knew what we were doing!

Dahlia and I are now closer than either of us could have possibly imagined, and although she has seen me at my absolute worst, we are all the better because of it. We know that together we are strong enough to handle anything life throws at us, and try to take full advantage of what life has to offer. We both work hard, and make spending time together a true priority.

Questions Unanswered

You wait, and you wonder
Is tonight the night?
Will I sleep in peace
Or toss and turn, and fear, and remember?

I'm fine, aren't I?
Then why can't my mind stop racing? And reliving. And remembering.
What's wrong with loud noises? And crowds? And driving in traffic?
And what the hell am I crying about anyway?

Help others, and you will help yourself.
But who am I really helping? Am I the punchline of a joke?
It takes time to heal, but who has the time?
I think my head's above the water, but maybe I'm too far down to know.

Take care of your family, your personal fireteam.
Together, you can sleep.
No re-enactments, no repeats, no missing pieces.
I can't wait for peace.

–Justin Constantine
Lieutenant Colonel, U. S. Marines (Reserves)

Dahlia and Justin walking down the aisle in 2008

I am Justin Constantine. Dahlia and I almost lost each other once, and neither of us will ever forget what that felt like.

Chase's Story

I was born Chase Cooper in Boise, Idaho. When I was 6 months old, my parents got divorced, so my mom moved me up to Seattle near mom's older sister, Jami. We lived in Woodenville, Washington in a trailer park adjacent to my grandparents. My mom worked, and I was too young to go to school, so my grandparents watched me. My grandfather became like a father to me, and I developed a deep love and appreciation for him. My father was still around, but I don't remember seeing him that often. I don't remember times as tough when I was a child, but I can well imagine that they were for my mother. A single mom with two kids living in a trailer park on one income is no easy life.

When I got a little older, my mother remarried, and my sister and I moved to North Seattle into an apartment complex. It wasn't the greatest neighborhood in the world. Things still seemed to be tight financially. I remember us shopping at the Salvation Army for clothes, and I can't remember my mother ever going clothes shopping for herself. We were always mom's number one priority. Luckily my mother had a wealthy older sister who sent my mom hand-me-down clothes.

When I was 12 years old, things started to pick up financially, I assumed, because we moved into a great neighborhood in Kenmore, Washington. This was where I had my first crush on a neighborhood girl, and we actually dated all the way through high school. I attended a private school for a brief time. Unfortunately, though, that did not work out too well for me, because I was expelled and suspended from that institution and from several other schools.

My mom couldn't handle me any more, so she sent me to live with my father in Kirkland, Washington, whom I did not get along with at the time. We really had no relationship. All we did was yell at each other. Surprisingly, though, I got into less trouble at public school and did better school-wise.

Traumatic experiences aren't new to me. When I was in the seventh grade, my father had me for the weekend and he and I were on the way to my sister's volleyball game when we were struck on our blindside by another vehicle. The last thing I remember is my dad saying, "Hang on." Our car flipped about five times before stopping. People called in the accident as a DOA (dead on arrival). We were not expected to survive such an extreme crash, but we did. My right knee got torn open, and my dad hurt his neck pretty severely. Thank God for seat belts!

During my sophomore year of high school, my father made the ridiculous decision to move my step-mom and me to our summer vacation spot, McCall, Idaho. Going from a big city to a small community (population: 2000) is a huge culture shock for anyone. I resented my father for doing that to me for a long time. Luckily, I was only there for my sophomore and junior year.

When my senior year came around, we moved to Boise, Idaho. I attended Boise High School. It was the best year of my life. It was rich with good friends, good experiences, and fun times. Towards the end of my senior year, my father and I were fighting so much that I ended up moving out on my own, getting my own place, and working until graduation. I was ready to "get out of Dodge," go see the world, and serve my country at the same time. So on September 28, 2000, I joined the U.S. Navy and said goodbye to my past. I served on the USS John. C. Stennis in San Diego.

Chase (right) and two friends from his platoon before deploying

After September 11th, our group set off for a 7-month deployment to be one of the first battle groups to start bombing parts of Iraq and Afghanistan. I was an Aviation Boatswain's Mate and launched and recovered naval aircraft quickly and safely from the ship's flight deck. In the Navy, this is considered a most dangerous job. You always have to be aware of your surroundings because the wrong move could get you or someone else killed.

I left the Navy in 2003. The next six years were the best and the worst times of my life. On the positive side, I met the love of my life, Alicia Chanel Cooper and fathered two beautiful girls, Gracie and Lucie. On the negative side, I feel like I wasted several years just going from job to job when I should have tried to go back to school or rejoin the military.

In January 2010, two monumental things happened to me that brought me where I am today. My grandfather passed away, and two weeks later, I lost my job. Trying to find work in Boise was impossible, like trying to find a needle in a haystack. Boise is a great city, and an even better place to raise a family, but I knew that if I didn't make a change and do it soon, my family would suffer financially. I had no health insurance, so we were left with bills piling up because of the treatments for our six year-old daughter, who was born with cystic fibrosis, a rare lung and digestive disease. Her treatment expenses forced us to file for bankruptcy. It just seemed that things were spiraling downward, and there was no way out. I was collecting unemployment, which was not much, and my wife was working two jobs.

Since we couldn't afford childcare, I was pretty much a stay-at-home dad, and that is a hard thing for a man to do. Well, at least it was a hard thing for me to do. I have a great work ethic and need to keep busy. Being a stay-at-home dad is plenty of work, but not the kind that was bringing home a paycheck to support my family. I was very depressed, and in my eyes, I was at the end of my rope, so I decided to rejoin military life. I have always believed that the Lord makes all work out for the good, and my time at home was no exception. In retrospect, caring for my girls ended up a blessing because it gave me memories to comfort me when I rejoined the military and had to be away from home.

Since I had exited the Navy with a medical discharge, I needed some waivers to get back into the military. I needed to get back to doing what I could do well. I wanted to lead soldiers and make a difference in this world, even if it a little one. I told my wife that I could go back into the military and she seemed to agree. I wanted to make sure she understood, so I asked, "Are you sure, babe, because if I do this, I will most likely be getting deployed, and there is a war going on right now." She had to think about it for a while. Then she agreed it would be the best for us and for the kids. So my processing began. I headed to the army recruiter and started all the paperwork, tests, and waivers. I thought the process would have been much faster, but it ended up taking almost a year from start to finish.

During that time, I spent countless hours watching YouTube videos of firefights, studying our current situation overseas, and trying to mentally prepare myself for what might lay ahead. I had a good idea of what to expect in terms of the environment, and I could envision the possible situations that I might soon face. While watching these videos–which, in retrospect, I can say were 100-percent accurate–I paid close attention to the risk for injury I would face from improvised explosive devices (IEDs). I knew that getting shot was going to be an everyday occurrence, but bullets don't always strike with the devastating accuracy of well-positioned IEDs.

On October 5th, 2010, I left my family to go to Fort Sill's Warrior Transition Course Program, which is a one-month training course offered to prior-service military. After training, I was assigned to be a cannon crew member (Artillery). That school lasted three months. I would soon find out that all of my extensive training would be of little use where I was going.

Next I flew from Fort Sill to Fort Drum, the Army's most deployed unit. I didn't even get to check in with my unit before I found out that I would be deploying in about a month and a half. From what I heard, we were headed to the most dangerous place in Afghanistan. I honestly made peace in my heart with the prospect of getting killed in battle. Not knowing if I would come back, I spent as much time as possible expressing my love for family before the day of deployment.

On deployment day, many families came to the unit to say goodbye to their husbands, wives, and friends. It was surreal. The reality that we were going to war really hit sooner for me than it did for the others, I think, because I was quite a bit older than the rest of the men in my platoon. I didn't think the others fully realized where we were headed and what would

Chase saying goodbye to his daughter Gracie

await us, but I knew that they would, sooner or later. It was just a matter of time before those first shots would start to pop off.

Upon our troops' arrival, we started missions, which the other platoon handed over to us. Before each maneuver, our squad leader briefed us about our mission and destination. My squad leader appointed me a team leader, which meant that when we went out on a mission, I was responsible for the lives and movements of my group. I had to make sure we did the right thing and went the right way every time. It was a huge responsibility, but one that I knew I could handle. The first time we went outside the wire on a mission just to get to know the area, I was scared to death. With every step I took, I feared that I was going to step on an IED. It was beyond nerve-racking. The more we went out, the more I got comfortable, but I always remained very aware of my surroundings.

It was amazing to me that during our platoon's first few fire fights, I was not out on mission. Our sergeant had split the platoon into two squads, so that we would only have to go out on one mission a day, instead of two. When the first firefight began, I was back at the Change Over Point (COP) with my squad, while the other squad was out taking fire. It was a horrible feeling, because there was nothing we could do but watch from the guard towers and see our guys out there on the ground getting fired at and returning fire. I wished that I could have helped, but I was also glad and amazed that I was able to stay safe.

As time went on, things just seemed to get easier. We were accustomed to getting little sleep and being out on missions 24 to 36 hours at a time. Sometimes we slept in villages surrounded by IEDs that we had detected, and sometimes we slept on the ground with all of our gear. I became familiar with the terrain, the people, and my surroundings, but never forgot that danger surrounded us.

When April came around, I was selected along with Sergeant Chan to go via Black Hawk to Forward Operating Base, Pasab, Afghanistan for a weeklong class of training to operate a mine-detection system. The flight was amazing. You really got a good perspective on how people lived just by flying over them. The class lasted a week, but we didn't get back to the COP until 11 days later, so it was definitely a nice break! Once we returned, it was back to business as usual, which included four to five days of missions and then two days of standing guard every six hours. Sleep was a luxury.

I remember the first day of June. It was the end of the poppy season and the beginning of the fighting season. No matter what time or day, our squad didn't go anywhere without getting into a firefight. The enemy especially liked to hit us during sunset because our COP was east of the villages that we occupied. So as we would head back, they would shoot at us. We had trouble seeing them because of the sunset in our eyes. If we could, we would usually call in air support to suppress their fire because the enemy was scared to death of the Black Hawks.

June 5th, 2011 was a day that would turn my world upside down and change it for the best. The morning started off great. We went on a mission to a village that was about 200 meters from our COP. We wanted to talk to a village elder with which we lost communication for a few weeks. He seemed to be a valuable asset to us and was very open, telling us about the Taliban's movement. When we got to his compound he invited us inside, made us Chai tea, and shared his food. (Unlike the Taliban, the Afghani people are very hospitable.) While we enjoyed our tea, my squad leader and I played with all of the kids for about an hour. It was a great experience because it made me feel as if I were at home. Before I left home, my daughter had given me three silly bands to wear. While I was with a few of the kids, I had the interpreter tell them that my daughter gave me the bands, and I gave them to the children. They were so excited! After the meeting with the village elder, we ended up doing a search of the compound for any weapons or possible IEDs. After everything was clear, we headed back to the COP for some downtime.

The next mission had my heart in my stomach. For some reason, I knew something wasn't right. Our 2nd platoon had left for a mission to a village that was always a source of trouble. As they left the wire and made it about 200 meters towards the village, they started taking small arms fire as well as rocket propelled grenades (RPGs). Our mission at that point was to go around their position and set up a tactical control point at an Afghan National Army outpost, which was about 400 meters away. We wanted to make sure that no insurgents escaped down the road toward our Control

Chase and Afghan Army guys after a mission

Point. If that did happen, we were prepared to either apprehend the enemy or eliminate the threat.

Our squad set up our position by the Afghan National Army Compound and waited. While at our position, I searched for IEDs in the surrounding area. Luckily, I didn't find any. We were at out Tactical Control Point for a little over an hour when we got the call from 2nd Platoon that they had captured four Taliban insurgents. Our next mission was to march over a mile to their position and stay the night in the village because the platoon had found an unexploded ordinance (UXO) there. When we arrived at the village, my good friend Monroe and I were exhausted. We had walked that distance in the dark with night vision goggles that didn't work well. About 15 minutes after our arrival, we headed to the wheat field where 2nd platoon had found the UXO. We all walked in file formation for safety reasons. When we were only halfway there, we stopped and found another IED. They seemed to be everywhere. Just a few weeks earlier, we had detected 23 IEDs within a 100-meter radius. While the IED was marked, we sat down and rested, realizing that it was going to be a long night because Explosive Ordinance Disposal would not dispose of ordinance at night.

We started moving again toward the field. Lieutenant Quink and Staff Sergeant Policarpo were in front of me and Monroe was behind. When I arrived, I asked if it was cleared of any IEDs, and was told it was. So we proceeded toward my lieutenant and squad leader. Policarpo asked me to walk over to their position to look for any more IEDs that could be in the area. I tried to walk in their direction on the same path they had taken to be safe. I must not have recalled the path correctly, though, because as I was turning to my right to take off my backpack, I felt the pressure plate under my foot. They had set the pressure plate up to be able to take out a line formation. Had we been in a line formation walking in the opposite direction, the soldier in front would have stepped on it and the blast would have taken out the rest of his squad behind him. I stepped on it from the opposite direction, and the charge was directly underneath my lieutenant's feet. I took one fateful step. My ears were ringing so badly, I couldn't hear anything for a couple of seconds. I will never forget what I heard next. My lieutenant was screaming at the top of his lungs in agony. At that point I knew we were in trouble. I started feeling excruciating pain in my head, ear, neck and right arm. I had taken massive amounts of shrapnel and was covered in blood from head to toe. As I sat there trying to assess my wounds, all I could think about was dying right there in that field. I then started to get really dizzy but told myself not to pass out because if I did so I was afraid I would die. I then started to think about my wife and kids back home, and that somehow energized me and snapped me back into it.

My good friend Manley found me after I yelled for help and immediately started giving me combat lifesaving support. He put a tourniquet on my right arm to stop the bleeding and bandaged my neck. I had pieces of metal shrapnel sticking out of my neck and had pain on the right side of my abdomen and the top of my right arm and legs. I kept asking him what it looked like, and he continued to tell me it was not bad. Smoke Arangus then came and finished up for Manley. When the light hit and they took off my Kevlar, I looked down and noticed that I was drenched in blood from head to toe. I was amazed. I couldn't comprehend it all. Where did all that blood come from? Smoke asked me if I could get up and walk. I was hesitant at first, but I got my feet under me and stood up. I had another 50 meters to walk to get to the trucks. It felt like 1000 meters. With every step I took, I was waiting for an explosion to happen again. The chances of that happening were high.

Usually where there is one IED, there is another nearby. Every step was slow and calculated. Smoke had his arm around me to give me support as I walked. He kept telling me that I was going to make it, and it would be okay. I kept asking repeatedly along the way if it was clear. It was. When I got to the trucks, they had better light, and I got the rest of my wounds bandaged. The tourniquet was so tight at this point I couldn't feel my fingers. I had to loosen it. I knew from where I was hit on the location of my arm that there were no main arteries, so I knew the chance of bleeding out from that area was unlikely. I was more worried about my neck. They wrapped gauze around it, and within the next five minutes, the Black Hawk landed, and I was rushed with the injured to Kandahar Air Force Base for immediate surgery.

On the "bird" ride over there, I couldn't stop thinking about Lieutenant Quink. Was he dead? Did he lose any limbs? Were they able to stop the bleeding? Thought after thought rushed through my head, and I was in tremendous pain. It was surreal. How could this have happened to me? I thought I would always be the guy that would watch soldiers fall around me and be the ones to pick them up, but I guess the Lord had different plans for me. It just goes to show you that no matter how much you think you are in charge of your life, your destiny is not yours!

When we landed at KAF they immediately took Lieutenant Quink off the bird and rushed him to the ER. He had lost a lot of blood and both legs from the knees down. They then took me off and rushed me in as well. It was a blur. There was so much going on around me, yet I couldn't hear anything and my eyes were foggy. They tried talking to me, and I told them that they either needed to yell or get closer to me when they spoke. I was almost completely deaf. They started cutting off all my blood drenched clothes until I was completely naked so that they could assess my wounds and attend to them.

The only thing I was thinking about was my wife. I yelled for the nurse and told her I wanted to make a phone call right now before they did anything else. I wasn't going to let some officer call my wife eight hours after the fact to tell her that I was injured. They got a satellite phone and dialed her number for me. I pressed the phone as hard as I could against my left ear so I could try and hear her. She answered. I mumbled to her that there was an accident and I got hurt, but I was okay. She couldn't understand what I was saying, so I put her on the phone with the nurse who told her what the situation was. The only thing the nurse could tell her was that she didn't

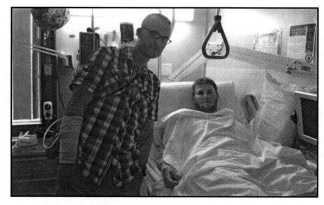

*Chase (left) with Lieutenant Tyson Quink, who lost his legs
in the same IED explosion that wounded Chase*

know the extent of my injuries and that I was heading straight into surgery. That is all the information she was given. She was hit with uncertainty, fear and disbelief. She knew how strong I was. She had faith that I would be okay, but every hour that passed was the longest of her life. Eight hours later she got a call from some officer telling her I was wounded in combat. I thank God I was able to reach her before she got that call.

The next few days were a mixture of blackouts and haze. When I woke up, I was in another hospital in northern Afghanistan with a two-star general presenting me my Purple Heart and my Combat Action Badge. I was so confused. They stuck around for a few minutes and were gone. Two of my other squad leaders, Staff Sergeant Cornell and Staff Sergeant George came there to visit me as well. That is whom I wanted to see. Not some general that just hands out awards, but the guys who were on the front lines with me. That meant so much more. They hung out for a bit and then let me get some rest. I was wiped out.

I had no strength, was groggy, and doped up on painkillers. A day or two went by, and I was ready and stable enough to leave the hospital and fly to the next one in Germany. I didn't care where we went, I just wanted to get out of that godforsaken country.

When we landed in Germany, I knew I was safe. I was there for about four or five days before being transferred to Walter Reed Army Medical Center in

Washington, D.C. I don't remember much of the flight home because I was sedated, but when we got there it was an amazing feeling. American soil, there is nothing like it! When you have had everything stripped away from you to go fight for your country and get hurt and are able to make it home, you appreciate America much more. Even though I was home, I was still looking and assessing my surroundings as if I was back in Afghanistan. Every building I passed made me look for the enemy. I remained on guard and always watchful.

I arrived at Walter Reed on June 11, 2011. The staffs of doctors and nurses were an amazing part of my recovery. I was blessed to have the best care the Army could offer. I couldn't have made it without them. I was so excited because the Army had arranged for my wife and the girls to arrive the following day. It was great to be back home with them. As they walked in the door, I will never forget the look on their faces. It wasn't happy. It wasn't sad. It was shock! I can see their look to this day. I had lost about 25 pounds and was on all kinds of painkillers. They didn't even know what to say to me. That painful moment of reunion made me question the rest of my career in the Army. I never wanted to put my family through that again, and I definitely didn't want the next time to be them showing up for my funeral.

It was time for my road to recovery and my transition to a different career to begin. I would find out that this process would not be easy. For the next six months, I worked on recovering from my injuries, having surgeries, and joining the Warrior Transition Unit at Walter Reed. From there it was a series of appointments after appointments to try and get my hand to work properly. The tendons were so damaged that my hand was constantly in a fist, and I was unable to straighten it out. I did occupational therapy for a month to get it to work even 50 percent. I was in pain on a daily basis and needed the assistance of my wife to do my daily living activities. She ended up being my non-medical attendant for three months. I had a wound vacuum-assisted closure on my arm, so I needed assistance with it in the shower, when drying off, when getting dressed, and when tying my shoes.

Those three months were rough for all of us because I had to make a major transition for the battlefield to safety with my family right away. My wife is an amazing woman. If I didn't have her help and support, I can't tell you where I would be right now. She truly is my backbone.

August finally came around and surgeries were over, finally. I ended up getting a skin graft on my arm because there wasn't enough skin to stitch it up. The IED had created a gigantic hole about three-inches wide and five-inches long.

The Army allowed me to take a vacation and go home for two weeks to relax and get away from everything. In retrospect, that ended up being not the greatest idea but parts of it were good. I was just too fresh from combat and my anxiety levels went through the roof. If anyone looked at me the wrong way, it was a problem. I tried to enjoy the rest of my time at home but really wanted to get back to Washington, D.C. I spent the rest of my time at Fort Belvoir in the barracks. My daily schedule included appointments and efforts to regain my sanity. At this point, I was alone. The family had to stay back home.

A couple months later my wife flew out to visit me. She stayed in my twin-size bed in my room with me for a week. That was rough! Before she left, my company commander approached me and asked me if I wanted to go closer to home or stay in Virginia. I quickly told him that I would appreciate being assigned closer to home, and within a week, I was on my way to Fort Lewis in Washington State. I ended up getting assigned to that Unit, and that is where I am currently stationed.

Just when I thought my life was over, all has changed and I realize that it has really just begun. I have been given a brand new shot at life with amazing opportunities thanks to the work of people who really care about my wellbeing. I am starting to see that my future is bright.

I am currently working on getting an internship with several different federal agencies, and I am starting my own support group for all the soldiers in my company. All I want to do is give back. So many people got me to where I am today, and the only thing I can do is try and help someone else get to the same place. There is hope. There is a future for all of us. I was blessed enough to not lose any limbs or my eyesight or my sanity. I want to show others that even with such ailments, you can still achieve your goals and build a bright future. It is so easy for any of us just to give up and get addicted to drugs and throw our lives down the toilet. The hard thing to do is the right thing.

The Bible says, "I can do all things through Christ who strengthens me." Believe it, and it will happen. Give God an inch, and He will give you a mile.

I look forward to sharing my story with the world if they will listen. I hope that I can inspire warriors who are down on their luck. I want them to have hope and hang on. I am now a role model for having hope and doing the right thing.

I have found through all this that I am not in charge. My platoon sergeant isn't in charge. God is. So change your mindset, have faith, have hope. Let go and let God. Even when things seem impossible, perseverance and resilience will carry you through, no matter the struggle. When times get hard and you have dark days, you can't allow those feelings to take over your mindset because it will consume you if you allow it too. You must stay strong and be a leader and set an example for others that may be going through the same struggles. Find a passion or an outlet that makes you happy and keeps you sane with others.

Daughter Gracie visiting Chase at Walter Reed Hospital

I am Chase Cooper and the bottom line is this: We are all human, full of flaws, and in this life together. The only thing we can do is learn from God, and from each other, and then share what we have learned.

Chad's Story

November 9, 2004 profoundly changed the course of my life. No childhood memories can even come close to the effect of that day, but many of them unknowingly prepared me for it. In many ways, the experiences of my youth helped me to develop the strength of character that I needed to rebuild my life after a traumatic injury in Iraq on that November day.

I grew up just outside Waynesboro, Virginia, in an area known as Hermitage. This part of Virginia is primarily rural with many small villages nestled near one another, running up and down the Shenandoah Valley. Waynesboro's population hovers around 20,000 residents.

My dad worked as a drafter and an estimator for a prominent construction company. He was well respected for what he did, and I remember him as always working on a side project or two for other people. He was an excellent craftsman and builder. More than anything else, I remember spending lots of time helping him to fix things for our neighbors. We would build new decks, repair broken pipes, and tinker with automobiles. My dad was even regarded as the "go to" guy when a bicycle broke down. No matter what the repair or building challenge, my dad would dig in and try, even if he didn't know what the next step would be.

I led an active life as a kid and participated in as many sports as I could. My sport of choice was baseball. I would play year-round with the kids in the neighborhood. We would gather in a nearby hayfield and play for hours. My dad would often be the pitcher and umpire for both teams. Looking back on it now (I am now a parent), I think my dad participated in the pick-up games to keep peace among the kids and to keep an eye on my brother and me. Whatever his motive, dad was always involved in my life, and he was a leader.

As best as I can remember, my mom worked, but I can't remember all the places. She had a passion for helping others, and I remember many times when I served as her sidekick at some function where we handed out food or volunteered at church. My mom also enjoyed singing. She and my aunt recorded and sold several albums together, and they used the proceeds for different charities. I remember many moments during my childhood that I shared with the two of them. When apart, mom and her sister were mild-mannered normal women, but when they were together, watch out, they would turn into a circus act. It never failed that when I was with this duo somewhere in public, mom and her sister relished the opportunity to embarrass the hell out of me. We might be getting groceries, and the two of them would break out in chorus to serenade me in the produce aisle.

My memories of mom left a distinctive mark. I didn't realize it when I was younger, but during my time in the military, my recall of her compassion and selflessness served me well. They became the model for my actions during stressful situations. Possessing the capacity to find humanity in the middle of war kept me from becoming riddled with post-traumatic stress disorder. Deep down, I feel fortunate to have survived and recovered as well as I have from the Iraq War, and I believe that my parents' influences played an important role.

My grandparents on my dad's side were also influential in my young life. I typically would visit them once or twice a week. My grandmother stood less than five feet tall, but she could cut you down to size if necessary. She was outspoken and direct. I remember her discipline the most. She had a lilac bush beside her house, and if my brother and I weren't behaving, she would tear into that bush with one swipe and get the largest whipping stick we had ever seen. Looking back on it, I don't recall that she ever used one on us because we usually calmed down before her blood boiled.

My grandfather was the opposite of my grandmother, as opposite as he could be. He was tall and thin and was very selective with his words. He was a World War II veteran, and he received a Purple Heart twice. It wasn't until he passed away that I learned the story of his second Purple Heart. My grandfather was the sole survivor of a tank explosion, which left him with severe burns all over his body.

Neither he nor my grandmother ever spoke about the War. They both seemed to understand its place in their lives, and they didn't need to revisit it every Sunday when I was around. Listening to my dad and uncle speak about my grandfather, I got the impression that he was a lot like my dad. He was the neighborhood handyman, and he never liked having someone else doing repair work for him; he was willing to try anything.

My grandparents enjoyed camping during the summer, and they would take my brother and me with them. Some of my favorite childhood memories are from those trips. There is a state park about two hours away from my boyhood home. It has a large lake and lakeside campsites all around it. Every summer, it seemed, my grandparents would bring my brother and me along with them and go there. We would swim, fish, catch salamanders, cook out, and listen to music. I especially remember the early mornings when I went out on the boat to fish on the lake. My grandfather was a pretty good fisherman, and we would spend all day on the lake; sometimes we caught fish, other times we didn't. Catching fish did not matter to me because being outdoors in majestic scenery was enough.

My childhood was not without adversity, however. It had a few roadblocks. My parents divorced when I was thirteen and my brother was ten. Overall, though, I believe my memories of childhood had a positive effect on my character development. My parents and grandparents all taught me about working hard, sacrificing for others, and showing leadership. I copied their good habits, and it helped me to build my character and prepare well for situations I would later face as a Marine.

After leaving college, I felt it was time to find a suitable job that would allow me some time to think and find my next "adventure." (I had held a job or some sort since turning age 15.) My mom called me one day out of the blue and asked if I was looking for work. I told her that I was interested in finding a job, but I thought it was strange for her to be asking. She was working for a local church at the time and someone had called her looking to hire someone reputable, so she passed my name along. I interviewed for the position and within a few days, I was working for a locally owned office supply store.

I delivered office products to area businesses. This included all kinds of office furniture. I quickly learned the value of bending at the waist to minimize lower back stiffness. I enjoyed the job, but more importantly, I enjoyed the people with whom I worked. The business was small, but it had a loyal following. I worked alongside another delivery driver whose name was Donald Rudd.

Donald was several years older than I was, but he would work circles around me if I weren't careful. He always seemed two steps ahead of me, and he was always thinking about the plan for the day and how he could work more efficiently. This captured my attention. Donald always came to work with a smile on his face and a work ethic that rivaled any I had ever seen. As I got to know him better, I found out that he had been a United States Marine, an infantryman. At my request, we talked endlessly about his military experience. He would share his stories about boot camp and the training he received. He spoke of all the different places he had been and of the missions he completed. He talked about the bond he forged with his fellow Marines, and the sacrifices he was willing to make for them. Donald was a strong Christian man, and the stories I remember most about his military experiences were those surrounding helping others. His most memorable moments weren't always to search and destroy, but to aid and help others. This contrasted with everything I thought about the military and peaked my interest even more.

As time went on, I found myself thinking more and more about a military career. I had taken a weightlifting class during college and had gotten hooked on fitness. I remember going to the gym and hopping on the treadmill to see what distance I could handle and what speed I could achieve in a three-mile run. Before long, I was keeping a diary of my progress and

*Chad (second row, second from left, with arms crossed) and fellow Marines
with one of the largest weapons caches they found*

was matching my performances with the Marine Corps standards. I became
increasingly focused on activities of fitness that would make me excel in the
military. I was totally hooked! I pushed myself past the point of exhaustion
day in and day out. Donald noticed my enthusiasm and encouraged me to
continue to push myself. He told me that my mental state would be more
important that my physical condition. He told me that if I were to join the
Marines, I would need a strong mind that could cope with stress, because
my body would follow whatever my mind held as its goal. I took his advice
to heart and began reading different publications on leadership and mental
toughness. I read whatever I could get my hands on. I kept an open mind
about what the materials were telling me and tried to absorb any new lessons
and ideas that were helpful.

All of these activities lasted only a few short months before I committed
myself to join the Marine Corps. I remember walking into the recruiter's
office on December 14, 1999, and having a short conversation with the
recruiter. I walked up to his desk and told him who I was and what I was
there to do. Over the next two weeks, I took the entrance exam and got all
of my medical examinations out of the way. Once that was completed, I was
scheduled to report to boot camp two days after Christmas. Over the Christmas holiday, I caught strep throat. I felt like hell the entire weekend and
contemplated calling the recruiter and asking if I could delay my departure

a week. I dismissed this thought and the next week, I found myself traveling to South Carolina with a van full of new recruits.

The ride was long and quiet. Everyone was anxious about what would come next. I remember that we stopped to eat at a Golden Corral, and none of us really ate anything; we all just poked at our food. Food was the last thing on our minds.

We arrived at Parris Island sometime during the night. I was sitting next to the door in the van. I remember being trampled on when the drill instructor opened the door. Absolutely every person in that van wanted off first, and I couldn't get out of the way for all of them. I ended up falling on my face and being yanked to my feet all the while being screamed at for not moving quickly enough.

Boot camp was an eye-opening experience. I had trained hard prior to my enlistment, so the physical training was no problem for me. However, the mental aspect was a challenge. I was the guide for the platoon. This meant that I was held responsible for my platoon as a whole, and I bore some level of punishment for any mistakes that were made. Early on, paying for everyone else's mistakes pissed me off and wore me out. I was always tired and hungry. But over time, I began to realize that leadership involves these types of sacrifices, and rather than feeling sorry for myself, I tried to make changes within the platoon. My strategy paid off, and the platoon learned to work together and sacrifice for each other to get through. I remember having a "normal" conversation after graduating with the senior drill instructor, and he mentioned that our platoon was one of the best he had ever had, and that my leadership was one of the ingredients for our success. Granted, I didn't do it alone. There were plenty of other people involved. I had a great support network of guys whom I could rely upon to get us out of a pinch by using all kinds of skills.

After boot camp came combat school and then training in Military Occupation Specialties (called MOS). My MOS was in the transportation field. I learned all about the military fleet and became certified to operate many of the vehicles within it. I enjoyed the job because I interacted with many different levels of leadership and assisted many with their training goals and general logistics.

I will now fast-forward to my last year of service. Operation Iraqi Freedom had been in full swing for roughly 18 months. I had come to terms with the fact that I might not be called to serve overseas, and I had made peace with that, knowing that I had served and done all I could do up to that point. As fate would have it, I received word about my unit's activation during the summer of 2004. My wife Kascie and I had just purchased our first home, and we were still getting paint on the walls and moving our furniture into place. In fact, I don't ever remember having time to mail my first mortgage payment before we shipped out.

I was attached to a company of combat engineers at the time of my activation. I was a part of the headquarters platoon within the unit. My platoon consisted of all MOSs that weren't combat engineers. Prior to shipping out, my platoon was divided among the engineering platoons, based on their needs. I ended up being placed with the first platoon and was heading over to Iraq. I remember those days following my new assignment as being very hectic. I was working for a new boss and was trying not to get into anyone's way; it was stressful.

Prior to leaving the United States, my unit was flown to Camp Pendleton, California, for several weeks of enhanced combat training. The atmosphere surrounding this training was intense. Everyone knew that the drills we were performing were in preparation for similar activities that we would be doing over in Iraq. Our focus was simple: become as proficient as possible with every task at hand so that everybody would come home in one piece. I took this mentality to heart. I was one of only a handful of Marines tasked with getting all of us from point A to B. I knew that I would need to be familiar with all types of equipment because I had no idea what types of equipment would already be in the country awaiting my arrival. So I spent many extra hours going over all makes and models of equipment in the local motor pool. I questioned seasoned mechanics about the possible equipment failures that I might encounter and asked what it would take to get the equipment back up and running. I learned a lot in those few weeks, and by the time we were ready to depart, I felt as comfortable as ever with my role in the platoon.

About two weeks prior to my departure, I learned that my wife Kascie was pregnant with our first child. I was totally shocked with the news. I was both excited and nervous about leaving her at home alone to deal with the pregnancy. The two of us did the best we could to console one another, as I was not allowed to return home. Surprisingly enough, my wife took things in stride, and we communicated back and forth about the baby via mail.

We left home on a gigantic aircraft that carried my platoon along with several other military personnel. The flight was long and uncomfortable; I was just too anxious, I suppose. We had a layover in Germany while the plane refueled, and then it was off to Iraq.

I remember landing in Iraq and stepping off the airplane and becoming lightheaded because of the heat. When I exited the aircraft, it was like the door was lined with a hundred hair dryers all turned on at once. I instantly started to sweat profusely. Dear God, the place was hot! I remember one guy telling us not to lay our rifles down in the direct sunlight because they would become too hot to pick back up in an emergency. I tested that warning once or twice, and sure enough, the rifle barrel could actually get too hot to handle.

After one more plane ride and a long convoy ride in the back of a 5-ton, we arrived at Camp Abu Ghraib, which was a part of Camp Fallujah located just up the road. The camp was fairly small and consisted of several small and medium-sized one-level dwellings where Marines lived and worked. All but six Marines in my platoon stayed in one room that measured roughly 20 feet by 30 feet. There were two windows in the room, but they had been boarded up and sand bags had been placed on the outside walls to protect everyone from mortar fire. Things were beyond cramped! We were constantly crawling over each other. We learned very quickly the value of deodorant. Every man lived out of his sea bag; each was constantly pulling equipment out and putting equipment back. Looking back, I can't believe we didn't lose more stuff than we did.

We also acquired an area, a small lot that contained all of our motorized equipment. Being engineers, we fabricated our own "command center" along one side of the lot. We first started with a wooden structure and reinforced the outside with Hesco multi-cellular defense barriers and sandbags. The new building was impressive given the conditions we were given. It was also the envy of everyone in the camp. It was rumored that the commanding officer requested we move out and he move in, but that didn't happen. We utilized the building for all sorts of activities. The building's main purpose was to give us an area where we could plan for missions and compose our gear.

After taking roughly two weeks to settle in, we began our operations. At first, we went on patrols with Marines who were leaving. They taught us about our area of operations and the various routes within it. They also pointed out the areas we needed to watch carefully. It was during these conversations that the magnitude of the situation finally hit home. We were traveling in small convoys all over the place, and we were encountering all kinds of people.

I was immediately struck with how the society seemed divided between the poor and wealthy. It was nothing to travel through a village and see 500 square-foot mud huts sitting directly adjacent to 4,000 square-foot two-story mansions that were beautifully adorned with colorful tiles. Aside from the occasional starkness between houses, all the buildings were constructed from the same materials and looked the same. It took a long time before I could recognize businesses and marketplaces. There wasn't much infrastructure except for structures dealing with water; everyone had a shared interest in keeping the water flowing. I remember many of the routes we traveled were adjacent to waterways of some sort. Depending on where you were, the roads were primarily dirt, but we did travel on some paved highways.

No matter what type of road we traveled upon, the threat of roadside bombs was ever present. We encountered improvised explosive devices (IEDs) buried under pavement, in piles of rubble dumped on the side of the road, in trashcans, and in ditches. There were few places without them.

Our area of operations was large and included remote villages, the Abu Ghraib prison, and the City of Fallujah. The diversity of the region kept us hopping. I can't remember a day when shots weren't being fired. There was always something happening: a roadside bomb hitting a convoy, a cache of weapons or explosives being found, fortified positions being mortar attacked, equipment breaking down in the middle of nowhere, improvised explosive devices (IEDs) going off along the roadway, or someone attacking the Abu Ghraib prison via vehicle or on foot. In short, any day you were on patrol meant it could be your last day on earth.

Marines in Chad's platoon are about to execute a "controlled blast" atop several weapons caches that were confiscated while on patrol. What is seen in the picture took less than two weeks to uncover; weapons were in abundance.

The city of Fallujah was robust and consisted of roughly 300,000 citizens. Many of problems we experienced with rogue gunfire, mortar attacks, and IED manufacturing occurred within this city. Early on, we were not allowed to enter the city. But by November 2004, the decision was made that Fallujah was harboring many extremists who were targeting Marine strongholds and threatening volunteer soldiers of the Iraqi National Guard. This disruption of operations prompted military leadership to develop an offensive plan that called for coalition forces to enter the city and rid it of extremist cells and add much needed stability to the region.

News of the offensive plan spread quickly and, before I knew it, my platoon was involved in providing support to the infantry. We were divided up into specialized teams capable of handling explosives, breaching, and dealing with the makeshift bombs that we encountered along the way. Because of our platoon's skills, we served different infantry platoons. When we received word that we wouldn't be entering the city together, our platoon was faced with saying our final goodbyes to each other early. I remember sitting in our staging area about to leave, and hugging and shaking hands with several Marines in the platoon. Deep down, I knew the battle we were about to wage would not afford all us a safe return home.

Up to this point, I had very limited contact with my family back home. The mail would run sporadically whenever conditions were safe enough to transport items, and getting successful computer access was like playing the lottery: there was a one in a million chances that the network was functional. Even when it was functional, guys would have to wait for hours on end to get ten minutes of access. I almost viewed computers as a liability given these long wait times. I knew Marines who were getting only a couple of hours of sleep each day because they stayed awake waiting for their turn at the computer. These guys were putting my life at risk when they were on patrol and were tired. Nevertheless, I couldn't blame them for wanting to reconnect with home.

Receiving letters or email was the best feeling. Rather than waste time waiting on computers, I wrote letters at all opportunities to do so. This served me well. My wife did the same. She sent letters almost every day. Our letters to each other talked about our daily lives, and she kept me up to date on the condition of our baby and reported on her progress through her pregnancy. I kept my letters simple and didn't talk about all the "adventures." My family also sent care packages when I wrote that I needed something. I would get things like protein bars, razors, and magazines. Receiving these items was definitely a blessing.

The oddest items I requested were a bottle of window cleaner and a bag full of sockets and wrenches. Believe it or not, the desert is a dusty place. The windows on our equipment would get absolutely caked with dust to the point that visibility was just a few yards in front of you. Before every mission, I would clean every windshield of every vehicle that was going to be used. In some strange way, I felt like a clean windshield was as important to our success as having a clean weapon. Tools were in short supply—you had to make do with what you had or just do without—and I did not want to be stranded in the middle of nowhere and need a 10mm wrench, so I wrote to my dad and explained my situation. My dad whipped together everything I needed and sent it as fast as he could. That small satchel of tools saved my ass more than once!

Without going into too much detail about our strategy for the offensive into the city, the basic premise was to start on one side and work our way through to the other. The city would be surrounded at all of the entrance and exit routes, to ensure no unwanted personnel could enter, and no unwanted personnel could escape. The battle began during the hours of darkness and during the first few hours, I remember it rained. The rain was horrible. It made the ground as slick as if there were two inches of ice on it. Furthermore, the mud was super sticky; it got everywhere you didn't want it to be. I remember that the bulletproof windshield on my Hummer (humvee) was much thicker than the conventional windshield that originally came on the vehicle. The bulletproof windshield kits didn't come with windshield-wiper arm extensions. This meant that the windshield wiper barely fit over the bulletproof glass and, in many cases, the wiper arms were never reinstalled. Luckily for me, I reinstalled my wiper arm, however, when I turned the wipers on, the wiper arm fell off. As if going into battle isn't stressful enough, I was trying to get there by driving at night, wearing night vision goggles, following a bulldozer in the rain, with a broken windshield wiper, and a windshield completely covered in sticky mud. As you may have guessed, I was "up shit creek without a paddle." Reflecting back, I remember stopping the Hummer and crawling around in the mud searching for the wiper arm; all the while, gunfire was overhead and the battle was in full swing. At the last second, I found the wiper blade and jammed it back on the wiper arm post. Had I not found the wiper, I was ready to tell one of the Marines to ride on the hood and use their shirtsleeve to wipe the windshield. It was very surreal at the time. How could one measly wiper blade disrupt the whole operation? It was kind of funny how such a small detail mattered so much.

As stated before, the plan of attack called for us to move from one side of the city to the other. I remember driving a few city blocks until we reached the route that we needed to clear. As I made a right hand turn onto the street, a loud explosion burst through the street in front of us. An insurgent had fired a rocket-propelled grenade at some of the Marines as they were about to enter a house. Here again, was another defining moment for me. I stared down the long run of city blocks ahead of us and realized that our advancement through the city would not come easy. Absolutely every room of every house, every street corner, every out-building, absolutely everything had to be checked. Sure enough, we found caches of weapons in bathrooms, under blankets, and on rooftops. Drugs were also prevalent. The insurgents had been in control of the city for months and knew we were coming. Rather than surrender, they would fight to their death. To give them superhuman stamina, they injected themselves with what appeared to be phencyclidine (PCP) and then attacked coalition forces. I remember finding a drawer full of syringes inside a school, all filled and ready to go. There must have been fifty syringes in one drawer alone. I remember thinking that we were fighting against an enemy that somehow knew they were going to lose, and they prepared to fight until the bitter end.

By the time we had made our way through one-third of the city, we had encountered endless insurgent attacks, found multiple weapons, and had taken some heavy losses. I was getting tired, and the end was nowhere in site. We had made our way to a two-story school when we received word over the radio that we needed to halt our advancement. The Infantrymen immediately rushed the school and secured the premises. We positioned all the vehicles from the convoy within the courtyard of the school in different areas to give us additional protection against outside attacks. I remember parking our Hummer on top of a trash pile that had to be at least three feet high. There were dozens of full trash bags thrown in one corner of the courtyard, and it appeared they had been there for weeks. I remember once we stopped, the flies immediately swarmed us and were everywhere. There were literally thousands and thousands of flies all over us. It was so bad that we grabbed only our weapons and ran into the school.

Once inside, our first objective was to set up automatic weapon positions. We had one automatic weapon in our squad, and I volunteered to assist the Marine in setting up his position on the second floor of the school. We grabbed everything we needed and followed some Marines up a flight of steps to the second floor. As we entered the room to set up our weapon, a rocket propelled grenade exploded just outside the window. All of us hit the floor as the dust and debris filled the air. I remember looking up and seeing Marines rushing to their feet to get a look outside to identify the point from which the rocket had been fired. Some Marines were yelling out the window, in no uncertain terms, that the shooter couldn't hit the broad side of a barn.

I for one was elated that the shooter needed glasses. Amidst all this confusion, I got my Marine set up, and I went back downstairs.

My squad was sitting in a classroom that was full of desks. I checked in with them and then began scoping out the other parts of the school. I entered a room that appeared to be the principal's office. It was positioned off the main lobby of the school and had one window looking out into the courtyard. As I entered the room and peeped out the window, I noticed a shadow across the street ducking out of site in another two-story building. I froze in place as my eyes scanned and rescanned the window that caught my attention. I kept asking myself over and over again: Did I really saw what I thought I had seen? I ducked out of sight and positioned my rifle at the window waiting for the shadow to reappear.

As with so many insurgents, the enemy in Fallujah had home field advantage, and they were well prepared for our arrival. Many of the insurgents' strongholds were fortified and had alternate escape routes within them. Walls would have small holes cut in the bottom of them where someone could crawl through from room to room without being spotted. Weapons would be staged at every window, and multiple weapons would be left in rooms on every floor. In these cases, the insurgents would literally shoot and run. This simple strategy made the enemy incredibly fast, because they weren't loaded down with equipment. Believe me, running up and down staircases with an extra 40 pounds of gear can exhaust you in no time at all.

After several minutes went by, I still hadn't seen anything and hadn't finished clearing the room. Knowing that small satellite patrols of Marines had been dispatched in the area around the school, I left my position at the window and continued my investigation of the room. As best as I can remember, the room was small and fairly empty except for one old office desk sitting in the middle. I walked over to it and knelt down to inspect it for any suspicious items that may have been hidden in it. When I knelt down, I noticed a small copper wire poking out of the bottom cabinet. I got my knife out and carefully pried open the door. To my amazement, I was staring at a detonation device that was only lacking explosives. I could not believe that I was standing inside a school, looking inside an apparent teacher's desk, about to remove a device that was capable of killing a dozen people. I removed it and set it on the ground and took the buttock of my rifle and smashed it into a thousand pieces. Then I grabbed what I could and threw it out the window.

By this time, it was getting dark, and we were ordered to stay inside the school for the night and continue our mission in the morning. Given our rapid departure from our Hummers earlier in the day (due to the flies), we were running short on water and food. My squad decided that we would need four individuals to race out of the school to the Hummer and grab a case of meals-ready-to-eat (MREs) and a case of bottled water.

The plan sounded easy enough, but as we exited the school, gunfire broke out, and we didn't make it farther than 15 feet before we had to dive for cover. We advanced toward the Hummer until all of us were stacked along one side of it. We counted to three and the swarmed around to the backside. I jumped into the driver's side and got a map and water. The other three Marines tore into the gear, and grabbed more water and food. It was kind of comical in a way because as I crawled back out of the Hummer, all I saw were bottles of water flying in the air and boxes of MREs being chucked from the rear of the vehicle. When we got back into the school, we regrouped and looked at each other wondering where the water and food had gone. We all burst out in laughter because all of us ditched our gear and

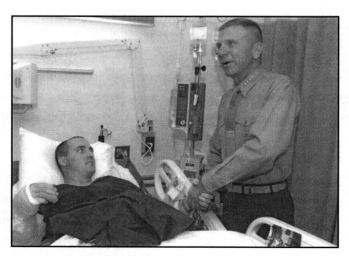

Chad receiving the Purple Heart from General Michael W. Hagee,
then Commandant of the Marine Corps

MREs and hauled ass back into the school. We raced back outside, grabbed what we had left behind, and raced back into the school.

Not long after we had finished eating, one of the staff sergeants for the infantrymen came to us and gave instructions to the M9 Armored Combat Earthmover (M9-ACE) driver to move his equipment and position it in front of the school house entranceway. This was to provide us added protection against sniper fire and rocket attacks. The M9-ACE was all-in-one style machine that resembled a small bulldozer with the top cut off it. It was covered in armor, and small-arms fire was no match for the steel plating on the outside of the machine. The machine was capable of bulldozing, scraping, and it even had a scraper bowl in the front that allowed it to do grading work if necessary. We received this machine and the driver just hours before leaving Camp Fallujah, and we used the machine constantly.

In most cases, we outnumbered the insurgents. This caused them to deploy tactics to try to bottleneck our movements through the city. They would set up roadblocks in different areas thinking we wouldn't push through them; they were dead wrong and our M9-ACE proved it. On many occasions, we would encounter a makeshift roadblock several hundred feet in front of us. We knew once we reached the roadblock, insurgents wanted us to stall just long enough for them to fire at our position. We would send the ACE in front of us to either inspect the roadblock or push it out of our way. I remember one roadblock was nothing more than old paint cans lined up across the intersection. When the ACE entered the intersection and began crushing the paint cans, the vehicle was slammed with gunfire. By utilizing the ACE to clear obstacles, we flushed out several insurgent positions that would have otherwise remained hidden, costing us our lives.

When we received the word to move the ACE in front of the school, I grabbed the driver and told him what needed to be done. I volunteered to go out to the courtyard wall and provide a watchful eye over the driver and his machine; little did I know that decision would change my life.

Both the driver and I raced out of the school, and he jumped into his machine, and I crouched down behind the courtyard wall. As I remember, the wall stood roughly ten feet tall and was comprised of large brick. The ACE driver pulled out into the street and came around to the front of the school where I was, and he drove through the courtyard wall doors. I was standing next to the doors when this happened, and the door across from me blew open and fell to the ground. The door closest to me swung open and dug into the dirt. As I recall, another Marine showed up and suggested that we try to reclose the doors to provide additional cover, so no one from the street could look directly into the schoolhouse entrance way and see what we were doing. We both began pushing on the door trying to pry it out of the dirt.

The next thing I remember was the wall falling on top of me. I had just enough time to raise my right arm to my face before hundreds of pounds of brick buried me from my neck down. Nearly two years later I got my hands on the after-action report. It stated that an explosion on the other side of the wall caused the wall to fall on top of me. All I remember is waking up in a cloud of dust and feeling immense pressure all over my body; seconds later, the pain hit. I had never felt pain like this before, and it was inescapable.

Prior to this moment in my life, my medical treatments consisted of getting a cavity fixed in one tooth and getting three stitches in my left thumb after a high school accident. I had always enjoyed perfect health, but now, I was trapped beneath rubble and couldn't move. Moments after the pain hit, I regained my bearings and immediately began screaming for someone to get me out. I remember looking up and seeing several Marines storming from the school. There was a large stone pillar across my chest that prevented me from being pulled from the rubble. I remember watching the first group of Marines trying to lift the pillar off of me, and they couldn't do it because it was too heavy. Instead, they had to set the pillar back down on top of me. In what seemed like forever, several more Marines arrived, and working together, they were able to lift the pillar up enough to drag me out.

From that moment on, shock set in, and my memory faded in and out of consciousness. I remember lying on the floor inside the entranceway to the school screaming in pain. I remember several Marines in my squad huddled over me trying to calm me down. Reflecting back, I know they were as scared as I was and were only trying to help me, but I was beyond the point of no return, and words brought little comfort. I remember speaking to one Marine about my ordeal that day and he stated that he pleaded with the Navy Corpsman to give me more pain medicine, and the Navy Corpsman replied that I had gotten the maximum dosage, and if I received just one more shot, I could have died right there from an overdose.

My injuries were extensive. I had suffered a broken right arm, a broken right leg, my pelvis was shattered, I had internal injuries in the groin, my right ring finger was crushed, my lower back was injured, and my whole right side was torn to pieces from the rubble.

Eventually, a Medivac was called in, but due to our location, that mode of exit was impossible. So I was placed on a stretcher and put on the back of a Hummer. I remember one Marine driving and the Navy Corpsman kneeling right beside me the whole ride. At times, he was lying across me to shield me from gunfire. I don't know how long it took to exit the city, but the ride was unbearable. Every bump in the road resonated through my body, especially my pelvis. I remember just before we stopped, the Corpsman yelled at the driver to slow down because I kept passing out due to the pain.

The Corpsman and I eventually arrived at a train station just outside the city that had been converted into a makeshift first aid station. I remember being carted into a room where medical personnel cut away my uniform and began tending to my injuries. I continued to go in and out of consciousness until I awoke to several Marines staring at me. To my amazement, I knew all of them; they were in my platoon. Their Hummer had broken down as the battle began, so they ditched it and helped guard the train station. When I arrived, they received the word and stayed with me the whole time. I can't tell you how good it felt to see those guys; I still get goose bumps thinking about it.

I don't know how long I was at the train station, but I left there in a helicopter along with three other men. The ride took a while, and we finally touched down at a field hospital that consisted of several high-tech tents and lots and lots of doctors. The only thing I remember at that location was being placed in a room with lots of other wounded guys, and seeing the doctors racing around, trying to treat us all. Again, I stayed at this location for a bit and then took another helicopter ride to a new hospital. By this time, the pain was so intense, all I could do was shut my eyes and focus on getting through minute by minute. I remember waking up inside a large hospital room, and I was the only individual in it. A few moments passed and a gentleman entered the room and explained to me where I was (which I don't remember) and what was going to happen. He stated that I was headed to Germany where I would be admitted to the Landstuhl Regional Medical Center. He was also carrying a large satellite phone with him and asked me if I had spoken to anyone back home. Being somewhat disoriented, I said that the thought hadn't crossed my mind, but I would try to pencil it in. I could tell by his reaction that he realized his mistake and stated that a phone call could wait. I agreed.

Sure enough, some time passed, and I was loaded onto a large military aircraft with dozens of other wounded service members. I was placed in a stretcher rack located down the center of the aircraft. Guys who could walk or sit, were positioned around the perimeter of the aircraft. The plane ride was long. I remember sleeping most of the flight and waking only to take more pain medications. I remember looking around and seeing blank stares on everyone's faces. The nurses looked like zombies; their eyes were blackened from the lack of sleep and the high stress of their jobs.

When we arrived in Germany, the weather was much cooler, and I remember feeling ice cold. When it came time for me to be unloaded from the plane, there were four individuals who grabbed my stretcher, one for each corner. As luck would have it, one of the people holding my head slipped and fell causing the other individual holding my head to fall. My stretcher smacked to the ground, and I thought I was going to meet Jesus right then and there. I felt pretty certain that 90 percent of my blood was replaced with morphine at that moment, but even that didn't dull the pain. I remember passing out to the sound of people leaning over me, apologizing over and over again; I awoke in a hospital bed.

I spent the next five days in Germany where I underwent surgery to my pelvis. When I was in recovery, I discovered that I had an external hip fixation device affixed to me to realign my fractured pelvis. It is quite a site to see a steel frame with giant screws sticking out of your stomach area. Aside from seeing my new hardware, I remember only one conversation and nothing else while in Germany. That conversation I had was with my mom. I remember trying to reach my wife and only getting her voicemail. My mom's phone number was the only number I could remember at that time, so the nurse dialed it for me. I remember speaking to my mom and anticipating that she would be very upset once she heard my voice. To my amazement, she was as calm and spoke slowly. My guess is the nurse spoke to her first and informed her of my mental state before handing the phone to me. I don't recall the topic of our conversation, but remember how calm my mom sounded. She spoke slowly and softly and reassured me that things were going to be fine, and she would let my wife know I was okay. In some small way, our conversation calmed my anxieties a bit knowing my family knew of my condition and that I was coming home soon. After five days in Germany, I was transferred to the Walter Reed National Military Medical Center in Bethesda, Maryland.

During the flight to the United States, I was awake more than I was asleep. I lay on my back staring at the stretcher above me. So many thoughts were running through my head. I was thinking about the Marines who saved my life and the Marines in my platoon who were left behind to continue pushing through Fallujah. I thought about my pregnant wife and all of the different challenges I would face with a newborn. I also thought about my current condition and all of the unknowns: Would I walk again? How long will it take to recover? Where would I stay?

My wandering mind was interrupted a different points in the flight due to nurses asking me how I felt and if I needed anything. At one point, I was handed a juice box and small bag of potato chips. I didn't have much of an appetite, but I was thirsty. I remember looking through the stretcher rack at the guy lying beside me. He, too, had been given a juice box and potato chips. His face was all bandaged up along with his hands. I opened my chips and gave them to him one by one until he was full. I will never forget how humbling that experience was. Here I was, fresh from the battlefield, bandaged up and coming home with my fellow comrades. I remember wondering if my grandfather went through the same experiences when he was wounded.

We landed in the United States and I remember that things happening quickly. Everyone on the plane was unloaded and driven to the National Naval Medical Center where medical personnel awaited our arrival. I was wheeled away and before I knew it, I had arrived in my room. There was another Marine in the bed next to me. We spoke briefly, but I was in too much pain to carry on a conversation. I remember how hard the bed felt and how much pain I felt in my hip and leg. By the next morning, the nursing staff had ordered me an airbed, and I was finally able to rest.

I don't know how much time passed before my family arrived at the hospital, but it couldn't have been more than a day or so. I remember seeing my wife for the first time, it was one of the greatest moments I have ever experienced. She was about four-months pregnant, and the baby was beginning to show. Seeing that for the first time was amazing. When she received word that I was injured, her employer immediately released her for two weeks to be with me. Furthermore, she received several monetary donations from local groups who paid all of her expenses while she stayed with me. My wife stayed by my bed from morning until night. Because I was confined to my bed, she gave me sponge baths, shaved my face, cut my food, and called the nurses when I needed them. I could not have asked for a better caregiver. When I think about it now, I still don't know how she did all of those things while being pregnant.

My parents and brother also came to visit. It was good to see them, but I could see that my condition worried them. I tried to keep my spirits up when they were around because I didn't want them worrying about me.

Life at Bethesda was a cross between heaven and hell. The medical staff worked tirelessly to take care of everyone. The hospital was a busy place with new patients arriving daily. They went above and beyond to meet our needs. In my case, I remember being in so much pain because of my pelvis. The nurses saw this and brought me extra pillows almost every night, so I could relieve the pain. I was also getting bedsores on the backs of my calves and ankles from lying in one place. Here again, they provided me with extra bath supplies to cleanse the sores and provide relief. That was the heaven part.

I had two teams of doctors that visited me once a day. Each team was comprised of several individuals. I remember when they would come in, everybody crowded around all sides of my bed. Usually only one or two doctors would speak, the rest listened. On one particular day, the first medical team arrived later than usual and the head doctor was carrying a large handful of paperwork. He discussed my injuries and my progression up to that point. He stated that because I was confined to lying on my back, my body was producing large amounts of scar tissue that would later inhibit my ability to walk as I had in

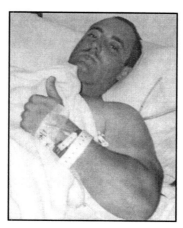

Chad recovering at the National Naval Medical Center

the past. My broken right leg was only bending four degrees and I couldn't lift either leg off the bed more than an inch or two. It was at this point that I began my long journey with physical therapy. This was the hell part.

I had two physical therapists who visited me twice a day and they concentrated on my right arm, my right leg, and my pelvis. Just before they arrived, my nurse would give me pain medication to deaden the pain. They would start on my arm first, beginning with the scar that ran from my elbow to my wrist. They would massage the areas around my scar and then flex my wrist forwards and backwards. I felt like my wrist would break. Once my arm was finished, they would focus on my pelvic area. They would have me do a series of leg lifts and stretching exercises. I didn't realize how stiff I could become after lying on my back for a long time. I didn't bend very well. The last part of every therapy session was directed towards my right leg. The therapist would raise my leg in the air while bending it. This wasn't too bad. Next came the tough part. He would place his hand under my knee joint and tell me to keep my leg extended for as long as I could, and then he would slowly lay my leg down on the bed. I did this for as long as I could bear the pain. My progress was marginal.

The scar tissue forming in my body was really limiting my ability to recover. I remember sinking further and further into despair until one night, I said a prayer and asked God to give me back the strength I no longer had.

The next day, a female physical therapist arrived. She wasn't my usual therapist. She was tall and built like a professional basketball player. Her voice didn't match her stature, as she was very soft spoken. She held a walker and large strap that was six-inches wide. She asked me if I was ready to walk. I looked at her with complete amazement and asked her to repeat herself. Again, she asked if I was ready to walk. Not knowing if she was misinformed, I explained my usual regimen and explained that I hadn't even been able to sit up, let alone step out of bed and walk. She calmly acknowledged what I was saying, but had only one goal in her mind, to get me walking.

So, the nurse came in, injected some pain meds into my IV and we began. The therapist put my bedrails down and repositioned my IV. She moved the walker close enough to reach it once I was standing. She then ran the strap under my back and tied it in a knot across my stomach. Next she slid my feet off the bed and helped me to sit up. I remember nearly passing out once I was upright. I hadn't been this way in weeks, and I guess my body has gotten accustomed to lying flat. She then placed her arms around my chest, and I hugged her as best I could. All at once, she lifted me from the bed and placed me on the floor. I couldn't believe it!! I was actually standing on my own two feet. I was pretty dizzy, but the therapist was right there assuring me that everything was all right. She then reached around my back and grabbed the strap. She directed me to begin walking by focusing on placing one foot in front of the other. By this time, my pain level was climbing quickly and the only thoughts that were going through my head were about getting back in bed. But the therapist wouldn't let me quit. She continued to encourage me to take my first step. Finally, I moved my left leg forward and set it down. Then I dragged my right leg forward. The therapist helped me move the walker forward and before I knew it, I had moved ten feet and was standing in the doorway of my room. She helped me turn around and go back to the bed. By this time, I couldn't hold myself up. She was literally holding me up by the strap. The last thing I remember is resting against the bed and passing out.

When I woke up, the therapist was gone and a nurse was checking my IV stand. She was smiling from ear to ear and congratulated me on my first steps. I never saw that therapist again but her visit taught me that I could one day walk. I believe my prayers were answered. God placed the therapist in my room that day to provide me with needed support at my darkest hour.

I spent a few more weeks at Bethesda and went through a few more surgeries. My wife had gone back to work, and she was traveling to see me every chance she could. The travel and pregnancy were taking their toll. I asked my case manager if I could be transferred to a hospital closer to her, so she wouldn't have to travel so far. Here again, God worked his magic. I was transferred to an inpatient rehab facility at the University of Virginia (UVA), only 35 minutes from our home.

UVA brought more challenges, but I was making progress. I could sit in a wheelchair. I could use the wheelchair to get to and from physical therapy. My physical therapist continued many of the exercises I began in Bethesda; she also introduced new ones. I began walking by using a set of parallel bars. I would ride my wheelchair between the two bars, then the therapist would help me stand up, and I would brace myself against the bars as she rolled the wheelchair out from under me. I would walk back and forth until I got tired. Some days I could last fifteen minutes; on other days, I was too tired to even stand up. Every day, though, my goal was the same—to get better.

Because I was closer to home, my wife visited me daily. We usually ate dinner together and watched TV. She would tell me what our growing baby was doing and what the doctors were saying. I was excited about the upcoming birth, but I was worried about how much I would be able to do to help her. Her parents kindly assured me that they could help her with baby care if I were still immobile.

While at UVA, I yearned to be home. I missed our home. I was asking the doctors every day to be released. Finally, I was discharged. Instead of returning to our home, I stayed with my in-laws. They graciously opened their home to me and to daily visits by my home healthcare team, which included a nurse, physical therapist, and occupational therapist. Over time, I regained strength and was able to walk around the house with an orthopedic cane that my wife gave me. And after several weeks passed, I was cleared to drive myself to outpatient rehabilitation.

When I began outpatient rehab, my right leg could only bend 10 to 15 degrees. My physical therapist recommended that I consult my orthopedic doctor who performed yet another surgery and improved my leg's ability to move. After that, I went back to physical therapy. After many days of stretching and strengthening exercises on my leg and hip, I regained almost 90 degrees of movement in my right leg.

My wife and I could finally move back into the home we had purchased just before my departure to Iraq. We tried our best to resume life as normal. I particularly remember one stretch of time during my recovery when I wasn't able to take a shower for seven weeks. When I was finally cleared to do so, my wife (seven-months pregnant) somehow managed to get me into my wheelchair and wheel me into a shower. I will be forever grateful to her for that moment. Feeling the hot water flow across my body was pure luxury.

Before long it was time for my wife to have our baby. It was kind of comical the day our daughter was born. I woke up around 5:30 a.m., and my wife was fully dressed and staring at me. She said it was time to get to the hospital. We moved quickly and just before lunchtime, our daughter Morgan was born. Our daughter was the most amazing little person I had ever seen. My wife handled the delivery like a pro. The next morning, while visiting my new family in the hospital, I was not feeling very well, and I told my wife that I needed to run downstairs to see my doctor. I had experienced a blockage from internal injuries, and the doctor rushed me to emergency surgery. Luckily, I had my cell phone with me. I called my wife's room and informed her what was going on and that I would see her later. When I woke up in the recovery room, my dad was there.

We brought Morgan home a few days later. The next few months were filled with long nights, dirty diapers, and lots of bottles. I was truly grateful to be able to part of my daughter's life and liked caring for her. I continued to go to therapy, and my wife continued to help me with the daily tasks that I couldn't do by myself. About a year passed and we decided to sell our house. We moved into a ranch-style house so everything could be on one level. The new neighborhood was nice, and our neighbors were very friendly. As Morgan began to get older, we decided to have a second child. In December of 2010, our son Tripp was born. Life got much busier again. When Tripp was 18 months old, we decided to look again for a house with more outside space where the kids could play. We found our current dream home just down the road. It is situated on almost six acres, and everything is still on one level. Both my wife and I enjoy the outdoors and this home provides us with endless possibilities.

My story is one about perseverance, redemption, and grace. In my youth, the good examples my parents and grandparents set for me gave me enough inner strength, discipline, and motivation to outlast the struggles that I later faced as a Marine. My training in the Marine Corps continued to build upon these qualities. My military training proved to me—and to many others—that deep within one's soul lies an incredible strength to cope with adversity. I remember, on countless occasions, being ready to give up and accept failure, but then I would think about my grandfather and everything he faced after being wounded. I reasoned that he recovered, so why couldn't I? Thinking about him always seemed to uplift my attitude enough to keep going. (I am sure he was reaching out to me from heaven.)

I am a Christian, and I believe that my successful recovery is linked to God's redemption of me. God's plans for me didn't call for my life to end on foreign soil. Instead, I believe he used my injuries to give me a mature life-focus, prepare me to be a good husband and father, and allow me to share my redemption story with others. I also think his grace continues to guide me as a father. And I am grateful for God's help because being a good parent is one of the toughest job on earth, and I need all the help I can get.

I simply can't end my story without focusing once again upon my loving wife Kascie. She sacrificed more than anyone to make sure that I got better. She was there at the beginning, when I needed someone to do practically everything. She stayed through every surgery and advocated for me, so that I received the best care possible. She made countless trips to pharmacies and home-health-care stores at all hours for me. She is also an exemplary mother and cook, so our family receives great love and excellent meals.

I hope that by reading my story and those of other warriors, readers can gain a better understanding of what it takes to recover successfully from traumatic injuries. In my case, recovery required mental toughness and determination, but it also required God's help, and the loving commitment of family members.

I am humbly reminded that many individuals choose to serve knowing that they may never return. Corporal Brad Arms was one of these brave warriors. I would like to honor the service of Corporal Brad Arms. He was among the Marines who pulled me from the rubble only to be shot and killed ten days later, when he rushed to assist another fallen comrade. Brad's hometown was near mine, and I remember when we first met and spoke about all the things we had in common. Brad was a hard worker who thrived under stressful situations. I am grateful for the heroism he displayed on the day I was injured.

After Brad was killed and I was transferred to the inpatient facility at the University of Virginia, Brad's father came to see me. I will never forget the moment he entered the room. For what seemed like forever, Brad's father stood at my doorstep and stared at me. Unsure of how much comfort my words would bring, I simply kept them to myself and stared back. Brad's father eventually sat down, and we spoke at length about my time with Brad and the deployment up to that point. Our conversations seemed to bring comfort to Brad's father. I hope they helped him to know that Brad made the ultimate sacrifice in an effort to bring stability and humanity to a place where lawlessness thrived. I know, without a shadow of doubt, that Brad's life made a difference. Brad, you are not forgotten.

And so, my life continues, but with new resolve. To all of the other wounded service members still in recovery, understand that you are not alone, and the quicker you allow others to help you, the faster your recovery will be. Never let a bad day kick your ass so hard that you lose focus. Dig deep and demonstrate your will to succeed to those around you. Recovery comes in small increments, and you will not heal overnight; it takes time. Listen to what your doctor's say and follow their advice, but don't let their expertise set your goals.

You are the master of your domain, and when you think you've hit rock bottom, you still have a choice: you can either go up, or go sideways. Remember, one choice will yield no progress, and the other will create new opportunities.

Chad and family on the farm in 2010

I am Chad Ellinger, and I am still here because others rose to the challenge to bring me back. For that, thank you will never be enough.

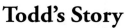

Todd's Story

While growing up in Arnold, Missouri, outside of St. Louis, I was a good athlete, a good boxer, and a bit of a daredevil, but in my mind, the risks I chose to take were reasonable risks. I would try things that my athletic talents could probably accomplish. And I was never reluctant to take the lead in an adventure, so, I guess I was always destined to be a Marine.

After graduating from high school, I worked for a while but found myself searching for a career that would ask more of me, something that would need 100 percent of my effort. I began considering military life and was attracted to the U.S. Marines.

My heroes were people like Rosa Parks and Martin Luther King who stepped outside of their comfort zones with little regard for the consequences because they believed in something—civil rights—much bigger than themselves and their local lives. This was the way I came to see the world, too, as a result of joining the Marines. Love of country was my passion. It was the big idea that appealed to my manliness while I was in my twenties. I was willing to pay any price to defend and protect my country and to preserve its international stature. For me, a career in the United States Military would enable me to do that.

Boot camp in the Marine Corps taught me a lot. Some of the guys arrived preoccupied with preserving their own cocky self-images, but they didn't stay that way for long. You can't be selfish and make it through the training. In the Marine Corps, there is no room for anything but teamwork. A squad, a unit, a platoon or a company can suffer from the bad actions of one member. So Marines train to believe that if one man fails, all fail. Everyone pays the price for mistakes made while in boot camp, because in battle, should the same thing happen—all will suffer for individual error. So we all trained hard and put 100 percent of our effort into our assignments because we knew that attention to detail and cohesiveness would keep us safe.

We all had a love-hate relationship for our drill instructor. I knew it was unreasonable to hate a man for doing his job, but I still hated him at times. Good came from the discomfort, though, because our shared dislike of him enabled us to become a "band of brothers." Drill instructors teach you to care for one another by demonstrating over and over again the price all will pay for failure of any kind. During boot camp, we all learned that we were only as strong as our weakest link. I was a team leader, so if any men on my team failed, I failed, and I went on the quarterdeck and asked my drill instructor to punish me along with my men.

During my Afghanistan tour, I loved being called "the old man" in charge of younger Marines. I was only age 25 when placed in charge of a squad, but that made me senior in status. We learned well to never leave a fellow-Marine behind, either in battle, or while serving in the rear. Even in peace, when Marines go on leave, or go home for the holidays, they invite their fellow-Marines to join them if their buddies have no family to visit.

It is said that war can have its "ribbon chasers," but I never met a single one in the Marines. For Marines, succeeding in war is not about glory. It is about trust. You learn later that the guy who is stays close to you in boot camp is also the guy who is watching your back in battle. You survive in combat because you can trust the man behind you.

Todd (third from left) and his squad on deployment in Afghanistan

And being a Marine brought me my spirited wife Crystal. She was also a Marine stationed at a nearby base in North Carolina. We met on the Internet and dated for several months before marrying in February 2009.

My first tour of duty went well. I served a tour with the Marines in Iraq in 2008. In 2009, I was sent to Afghanistan as leader of 12 Marines in the 1st Squad, 1st Platoon, Company F, and 2nd Battalion. But this time I was leaving a wife behind. I considered it a blessing that Crystal was a fellow-Marine because she could clearly understand what we faced and why we fought. If adversity came, I already knew that my wife was Marine-ready.

Right after our first wedding anniversary, the unthinkable happened. I was six months into my tour of duty when, on March 26, 2010, near the town of Lakari in southern Afghanistan, while leading my infantrymen during a routine security patrol, I was struck down by an improvised explosive device (IED). A crude, single-file bamboo bridge over a canal housed a buried IED consisting of over 40 pounds of explosives. It was a gory sight, even by war standards. My buddies described how my helmet and flak jacket were blown off and my bones and bowels were sticking out everywhere. My men and nearby Corpsman worked feverishly to tourniquet the bleeding and check my vital signs. Besides losing all four limbs, I endured shrapnel that passed through my jaw and exited through my cheek. My men later discovered my hand nearby, after they had put me on the "bird" en route to the hospital.

I don't remember much after the blast, but I do recall screaming loudly because I was in extreme anguish. I knew that parts of me were gone, but I had no idea of the extent of my injuries. I remember thinking two things: Try not to scream any more because it will scare my men; try to keep breathing, so I can see Crystal again.

I gave my country all four limbs that day¬—my right leg at the knee, my left leg just above the knee, my left arm at the wrist and my right arm at the elbow¬—and still managed to survive because of Marine loyalty and unwillingness to leave a man behind.

Crystal left the military in June 2009, so she was back in Kansas visiting her sisters when she received the news of my injury in battle. A sergeant major asked Crystal to be seated before telling her that I had been severely injured, was still alive, but was missing some limbs. Crystal insisted upon getting to me as quickly as possible, so she took a commercial flight to Landsthul, Germany, where I was being treated.

Crystal captured the Marine-tough spirit of our marriage by describing

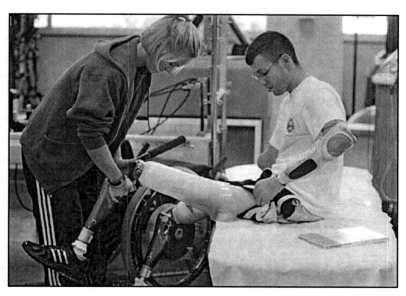

Todd and Crystal suiting up in the hospital

Todd and Crystal practicing putting

her thoughts this way, " It wasn't good, but to me, it was still Todd. His missing limbs didn't really affect me. I saw him breathing, and I thought: 'Okay, he's still alive. He's still with me.' "

From Germany, I was transferred to the National Naval Medical Center in Bethesda, Maryland. Crystal did not know what I knew of my injuries, and her biggest worry was whether or not I would lose hope, or would fight to regain a "new normal" life for us.

I woke up one night and told Crystal: "I don't know what's wrong."

"Do you want to know what's wrong?" she asked me.

When I responded, "Yes," she said, "Well, baby, you know you're missing your legs."

And I said, "Yeah, I know."

Then she cried and asked me, "Did you know you're missing both hands?"

I asked her, "Did anyone else get hurt?"

Crystal answered, "No."

"Good," I replied, and I went back to sleep.

From that moment onward, our rebuilding started. We now both knew what we faced, and we were resolved to surmount the odds together.

No one can possibly imagine what it is like to go from being a warrior to needing someone else to brush your teeth for you, help you use the toilet, help you eat, dress, bathe. The adjustments that I had to make were numerous and formidable, but not impossible. The key for Crystal and me was keeping a positive attitude. Crystal was right in her assessment of the situation when we met again in Bethesda, Maryland. There were two choices: One could take the path of hope, or go down the dark path of being a perpetual patient. We chose the path of hope and hard work.

In spite of advice that my recovery would take four years, we set a goal of getting out of rehabilitation within a year. My recovery would require me to learn how to use my mechanical hands, master my Nustep Machine, and even operate a motor vehicle one day. (Today I actually drive my own truck and boat.)

The adjustment to my mechanical hands required as much in terms of patience as it did dexterity. For me, it was like playing the crane-type game commonly found in amusement park arcades. While as a kid, I used to aim the claw and win a stuffed animal or prize, now I needed to coerce a gadget capable of delivering 25-pounds of pinching pressure to gently open a can of soda or a bottle of pills. Winning the game was now my ticket to independence.

I learned how to "win the prize" with my mechanical hands and moved on to walking with my artificial limbs. Two years later, I could be found going for a two-mile run using my Nustep Machine, a fine invention. I do this on the anniversary of my injury to remind myself that all of my limbs were sacrificed, but not my will to live nor my personality. The approval of passer-bys is not what I seek when running as a mechanical man. What keeps me going is the deep satisfaction I get from knowing that today, with Crystal at my side, I am still giving my best to serve family and country.

I do not like to think of my own story of rehabilitation in courageous terms. I did what I had to do. My choice was either to mope in bed, or get up and get at it. My first goal was to stand up, and then learn to walk, then run, and then become independent again. I just take one day at a time and live for the next day. I don't like being put on a pedestal because I am just being a good Marine.

I do think my wife's role in my rehabilitation was, and remains courageous. Crystal was not only at my side throughout my recovery, but she, like Rosa Parks and Martin Luther King, has done many things since my injury that required her to step outside of her comfort zone. She influenced the medical board process by testifying in Congress. She poured her heart out to them to improve the process and paperwork of rebuilding the lives of our wounded warriors.

Together Crystal and I continue to serve our country by sharing our successful recovery with newly wounded warriors so they, too, will choose the path of hope.

Todd and Crystal during the summer

We are Todd and Crystal Nicely. We both handle the rehabilitation like good Marines. We just take one breath at a time. One surgery at a time. One step at a time.

Brad's Story

While you are a midshipman at the Naval Academy you are required to memorize, among other things, the core values of the Navy. These values are Honor, Courage, and Commitment. For most of my Naval career, these were just words to be recited, or infrequently to be put at the bottom of an inspirational photograph, but now, as I look back at my life, I can see how these values have been an integral part of my character development.

My Reflections on Honor

If…
If you can keep your head when all about you
Are losing theirs and blaming it on you,
If you can trust yourself when all men doubt you,

But make allowance for their doubting too;
If you can wait and not be tired by waiting,
Or being lied about, don't deal in lies,
Or being hated, don't give way to hating,
And yet don't look too good, nor talk too wise:
If you can dream—and not make dreams your master,
If you can think—and not make thoughts your aim;
If you can meet with Triumph and Disaster
And treat those two impostors just the same;
If you can bear to hear the truth you've spoken
Twisted by knaves to make a trap for fools,
Or watch the things you gave your life to, broken,
And stoop and build 'em up with worn-out tools:
If you can make one heap of all your winnings
And risk it all on one turn of pitch-and-toss,
And lose, and start again at your beginnings
And never breathe a word about your loss;
If you can force your heart and nerve and sinew
To serve your turn long after they are gone,
And so hold on when there is nothing in you
Except the Will which says to them: "Hold on!"
If you can talk with crowds and keep your virtue,
Or walk with kings—nor lose the common touch,
If neither foes nor loving friends can hurt you,
If all men count with you, but none too much;
If you can fill the unforgiving minute
With sixty seconds' worth of distance run,
Yours is the Earth and everything that's in it,
And—which is more—you'll be a Man, my son!

—Rudyard Kipling, 1910
"If" poem from Rewards and Fairies

My understanding of honor is built upon the teachings of my father.

He was a very loving father, and a person of strong moral character. He took an early interest in imbuing me with a comprehensive understanding of virtue. I did not make this process easy on him. As his firstborn, and a child of very high energy, I felt compelled to challenge all his lessons through trial and error instead of taking him at his word. I often found myself in trouble, and each time, I was rewarded with a lecture. Now that I am older, I am supremely grateful that my father had the patience to put up with my shenanigans, to take the time to teach me right from wrong and the value of virtue.

From my early ages through adolescence, I perceived my father's great reverence for our flag and for the men who served under it. Had it not been for a rare genetic ailment, I am convinced that my father would have donned a United States Navy uniform as soon as a recruiter would have allowed him to sign his life away. His father and brother both had done so, and my father's upbringing was rich with the experiences of a Navy family traveling around the world as part of our country's great fleet. My father told me Navy stories about his father, about growing up in Japan, about how his brother went deep under the ocean in this thing called a submarine. I could see a

Brad learning to cane

gleam in his eye as he told me these stories, and I could feel his longing to be out on the sea aboard a giant grey warship. It was while hearing those stories that my own desire to serve the country began to take shape. My initial motive was simply to make my father proud. I also think that I was beginning to understand the virtue of honor.

My father's lessons permeated all aspects of my childhood. For him, even something as simple as playing catch was an opportunity to learn about seeking perfection and virtue. As we would toss the ball back and forth, my father was always coaching me with ways to improve. If I ever made a catch or throw that was inconsistent with his fundamentals, he was quick to critique my performance. There were certainly times where I felt that he was being nitpicky; however, over time, I learned to critique my own performance. And this mentality was not limited to playing catch. It began to trickle into all other aspects of my young life. The discipline I learned from my father through something as simple as playing catch largely shaped me into the "Type-A" personality that I am today.

When I was six-years-old, my family moved west from the swamps of Florida to the base of the Rockies. We made our new home in the then largely barren city of Colorado Springs. In retrospect, I believe my fondest memories of childhood all occurred there. From our home, I could easily see the Chapel of the Air Force Academy and the beautiful summit of Pike's Peak. If I looked slightly off to the west, I saw the antennas of North American Aerospace Defense Command (NORAD). During that time, George Herbert Walker Bush (Bush Sr.) was President, and General Herbert Norman Schwarzkopf, Jr. (Stormin' Norman) was all over the evening news as he led the US forces that stormed the deserts of Iraq. As we sat in our living room witnessing history unfold before us, my father taught me about the previous events that have shaped our armed forces and current military strategy. He used to allow me to stay up late on Monday nights so I could watch my favorite show, "Tour of Duty," a show about an Army platoon's endeavors in Vietnam. My dad explained the political conditions that led us to involvement in both Vietnam and Iraq, and he taught me about the progression of warfare from the trenches of World

Brad and sister Elyse before the Tampa Navy Ball in 2011

War I, all the way through to the guerilla tactics of the North Vietnamese War. As he lectured, I could sense his great admiration for our country's military heroes, and, in turn, I developed the same.

Even while still a young boy, I greatly desired to be a part of my father's stories, and this was reflected in everything I did. I watched the movie "Top Gun" repeatedly, and I built weapons out of LEGO parts. I went to air shows with my father and worshipped the engineering miracle that was the F-117 Stealth fighter. I went to Air Force football games, and I longed to be a part of the mass of students who were required to charge the field and do pushups each time their team scored.

As a child, I always held an image of a military future in my mind, but I didn't have specific goals until I visited the Naval Academy at age 15, during the summer of 1999. My uncle, who was serving as a Naval Judge Advocate General (a Naval lawyer) at the time, suggested he and I visit the campus merely as tourists. While walking the grounds of the historic school, I was enamored with its rich history and tradition. It wholly embodied my childhood image of who I wanted to be, and I fell in love with a Navy career at that moment. My dream of one day being part of the Brigade of Midshipmen became an integral part of my daily routine. I immediately signed up for their mailing list, and I poured through all the available information on the Academy's website. I found a candidate checklist and pinned it up on my corkboard at home. That checklist became my gospel over the next few years, and I followed it with the fervor of a Buddhist monk.

During the Christmas break of my senior year in high school, after returning home from a long and difficult swim practice, I received the Christmas gift of a lifetime. On the stoop of our house sat a FedEx envelope addressed to me with the return address of the U.S. Naval Academy. My hands trembled as I ripped open the envelope. Inside was a single piece of high-quality linen paper with a glossy emblem at the top. There were five paragraphs, but my eyes zeroed in on the only words of importance on the page. Near the bottom, the letter read "Welcome to the Brigade of Midshipmen Class of 2006!"

The next few months went by in a flash. I don't remember much of that time as my mind was elsewhere. I was mentally preparing for the rigors of Plebe Summer (Freshmen at the Naval Academy are referred to as "plebes," and the indoctrination period similar to "boot camp" is referred to as Plebe Summer), my departure from home for the first time, and my transition from a Florida boy into a Navy man. Inside I was terrified and elated at the same time; meanwhile, outside, I tried to appear as stoic and indifferent as possible.

I received another letter from the Naval Academy outlining exactly the procedures I needed to be familiar with for my induction. The letter clearly stated the expected attire for "Induction Day," affectionately called "I-Day." New plebes were to show up wearing a collared polo shirt of neutral color tucked into a pair of khaki trousers. Plebes were to show up wearing tennis shoes, as they would need them for the physical training they would endure each morning at sunrise. Plebes would be allowed to, but were not required to, bring a tennis racquet and a baseball glove. All other personal items would be confiscated.

This is exactly the way I showed up to the Naval Academy. While I truly was shocked when my upperclassmen began yelling, I was completely elated. I was finally going to become what I had always dreamed of being, a military man.

After approximately ten hours of hauling around large laundry bags of initial issue, and performing poor recitations of midshipman rates that I did not yet know (rates are a list of various items of naval history and basic military knowledge that plebes are required to commit to memory), the Class of 2006 was assembled in what is called "T-Court," named after the bronze statue of Tecumseh at one end. (Tecumseh was a Native American leader of the Shawnee and of a large tribal confederacy that opposed the United States during the War of 1812. He was respected as a true warrior by both sides of the conflict, and so he has become a symbol of strong will and determination.) It was at that assembly that the Superintendent acknowledged us as the Class of 2006 for the first time. Despite the fact that we were under strict guidance to sit at attention with our eyes straight forward "in the boat" as they say, I could not help but look around at my surroundings and smile. Before me was Bancroft Hall, where I was a new resident. Behind me were the academic buildings of one of the most respected institutions in the world. All around me were the best and the brightest, my peer group, and we were all here to serve. It was at that moment when I finally understood what honor was, and I beamed with pride at the realization that I was a part of it. I will remember that moment for the rest of my life.

My Reflections on Courage

"It is not the critic who counts: not the man who points out how the strong man stumbles or where the doer of deeds could have done better. The credit belongs to the man who is actually in the arena, whose face is marred by dust and sweat and blood, who strives valiantly, who errs and comes up short again and again–because there is no effort without error or shortcoming–but who knows the great enthusiasms, the great devotions, who spends himself for a worthy cause; who, at the best, knows, in the end, the triumph of high achievement, and who, at the worst, if he fails, at least he fails while daring greatly, so that his place shall never be with those cold and timid souls who knew neither victory nor defeat."

—Theodore Roosevelt
"Citizenship in a Republic,"
Speech at the Sorbonne, Paris, April 23, 1910

Swimming taught me the virtue of courage. My father was an extremely aquatically inclined individual. Born a child of a New York State champion back stroker in the 1930s, my father spent much of his time as a child and as a young adult swimming at the local community pool or bodysurfing at beaches all over the world. He was able to instill the same passion for water in each of his children, and, as a result, we spent a large part of our childhood in the same manner. When I was only 3 years old, my father would encourage me to dive to the bottom of the pool and retrieve such treasures as pennies or Batman action figures. By the time I was 11 years of age, I fancied myself a pretty good swimmer. This perception was shattered when my father took me to the local community pool to try out for the swim team. I had a decent freestyle, a passable backstroke, a terrible breaststroke, and a nonexistent butterfly stroke. A former Florida State University star linebacker, my new swim coach, looked unimpressed, but he agreed to allow me to start practicing. Humbled by the apparent swimming prowess of my new teammates, I realized that I had a long way to go. For the first time in my life, I was faced with a challenge and the outcome was unsure, so instead of getting discouraged, I ignited a small competitive flame deep inside and vowed that I would do whatever it took to not be the worst swimmer on that team. I swallowed my pride and donned a Speedo. I practiced six days a week, for at least an hour per day. At the end of each practice, I felt as though my arms were made of lead, and at times, it was a struggle to muster enough energy to eat my dinner before passing out exhausted and then getting up to do the same thing the next day.

Before long, I was no longer the worst swimmer on the team. Encouraged by my progress, I picked out specific targets, and set specific goals. Within a year, I reached my first age-group state qualification time. At that meet, I finished nearly last in every event I swam, which further fueled my small but growing competitive flame.

Soon after I began swimming, my siblings—a sister and two brothers— joined the team as well, and swimming became a family affair. We became obsessed. Dinner conversation, if anyone had the energy, always revolved around the pool. Swim meets took up almost every weekend. By the time I reached high school, I actually was the swimmer I had originally believed myself to be. That intrinsic competitive flame had become a forest fire, and any success I had achieved to that point was not good enough. I distinctly remember watching a pale, freakishly tall swimmer by the name of Tom Dolan earn a gold medal in the 400-meter individual medley (100 meters of each stroke) setting a world record in the process. Even as a 12-year-old kid, I got teary eyed when they raised the American flag and played the Star-Spangled Banner in honor of his achievement at the 1996 Summer Olympics. I didn't see any reason that I could not achieve the same in the coming years. I wrote the Olympic Trial qualification time on the brim of my favorite hat and started doing two practices a day.

Before my junior year of high school, my family moved, and my new high school happened to have a very competitive high school swim team. Early in the high school season, over a gargantuan Village Inn breakfast, my teammates hatched out a plan to win the High School State Meet. This was the pinnacle of team competition, and we had all the elements we needed to just eke out a victory over the "New England Patriots" of our division, St. Thomas Aquinas High School from Ft. Lauderdale. To win, every person on our team would need to swim their best times by a hefty margin, and we would have to have

Brad (right), with his brother Russell serving as his running guide,
at the Warrior Games in 2012

stellar relay performances. That being said, our collective competitive flames could have gotten a shuttle into orbit, so we went to work.

We ended up losing to St. Thomas in a heated meet that gives me goose bumps to recall. In spite of our overall loss, we all met our individual goals, and had amazing relay performances. Some of our records from that meet still stand to this day. Through a semester-long battle, my teammates and I established a brotherhood that can only be accomplished through shared sacrifice and dedication to each other and our mission. None of these things, however, made defeat any easier to swallow. Collectively, we silently went back to our double practices the following week, and shifted our focus to dreams of competing on the collegiate level, which might perhaps one-day springboard us to competition on the national level.

As a result of my efforts that year, I was able to reach a Junior-National-level time standard that landed me on the radar of exactly one Division I program, the U.S. Naval Academy. That was good enough for me, as I was, at this point, about three-quarters of the way down my checklist anyway.

As many high school athletes experience, I was initially blown away by collegiate swimming. The standard of performance was very high, the goals were lofty, and the team dynamic was even stronger than what I experienced on our state-runner-up high school team. Even as a bald-headed plebe, the Naval Academy swim team welcomed me and my classmates with open arms. Though my world had dynamically shifted, I found a great deal of comfort in the familiar intensity of swim practice and competition. Practice became a welcome reprieve from all of the yelling and rates that consumed much of our time back in the dorms. We commiserated, and strong bonds were established through our shared sacrifice of sleep and liberty. Due to the raised standard of performance, we all gained a healthy appreciation for each swimmer and his contribution to the efforts of the team. If one swimmer had a bad meet, that might be the difference between victory and defeat. So we were very supportive of each other, while at the same time, we kept each other humble with a healthy dose of good-natured ribbing.

Even though our curriculum required us to take somewhere in the realm of 20 credit-hours of leadership courses, I actually built my leadership foundation on my experiences at the pool. My heroes were the captains that led us through season after season. Even as a plebe, I recognized the value of such amazing leadership from such young men. No matter what high or the low our team was experiencing, the captain always seemed to know just the right thing to say. His behavior set a perfect example to emulate, and his confidence never faltered. Early in my time at the Naval Academy, I resolved to shape myself into such a leader. I was incredibly fortunate when I was able to put this to the test when I was nominated Team Captain for the 2005-2006 season.

While I was ecstatic about the opportunity to lead, I would be lying if I claimed to feel as though I deserved the honor. The weight of the team was now on my slender shoulders, and I was terrified of letting my teammates down. My fear of defeat and resolve to attain victory both gave me the confidence and motivation I needed to stand before my fellow-swimmers and lead them through the rigors of a long swim season. That year, we did not win our conference meet, and I personally swam terribly, yet it was the most rewarding year of my life. I have the utmost respect for the brotherhood of Navy swimmers, and to have spent four years in their company, and to finish my time among them as their captain, shaped me into the leader I have become.

After graduation in 2006, I left the swim team to join a new one. My new team was called Navy Explosive Ordinance Disposal (EOD). Again the standard of performance was raised, and the stakes of competition were elevated. As an EOD technician, my metric for success was no longer measured in time, but in terms of a much more dramatic metric of life vs. death. That being said, the team dynamic was largely unchanged. Once again, the bonds of brotherhood were established on our shared willingness to sacrifice for the benefit of others and our American way of life. We supported one another, while keeping each member humble by endlessly poking fun at shortcomings. As an Officer on my new team, I felt the same responsibilities as when I served as swim team captain at Navy. I needed to ensure that my boys received good care, that their motivations never waned, and that they were given a good example to follow. The professionalism of my new team largely didn't require an example; in fact, I found myself learning much more from my teammates than I could ever teach them.

Over the next six years, I had the privilege of serving with my new EOD team in support of both Operation Iraqi Freedom and Operation Enduring Freedom. We worked with some of the best operators in the world, including Army Special Forces, Rangers, Navy SEALs, and of course EOD technicians from all the other armed services. I have found uncanny parallels between the team dynamics that I experienced on the swim team and those on the battlefield. Obviously the intensity of these experiences are scaled differently, but there are certainly similarities. In both settings, the bonds between teammates are built upon shared appreciation for the sacrifice and dedication of each member. These bonds cannot be broken. My appreciation for these experiences of brotherhood developed my leadership, and they have allowed me to understand true courage.

My Reflections on Commitment

"Until one is committed, there is hesitancy, the chance to draw back, always ineffectiveness. Concerning all acts of initiative and creation, there is one elementary truth the ignorance of which kills countless ideas and splendid plans: that the moment one definitely commits oneself, then providence moves too. All sorts of things occur to help one that would never otherwise have occurred. A whole stream of events issues from the decision, raising in ones favor all manner of unforeseen incidents, meetings and material assistance which no man could have dreamed would have come his way."

—William Hutchinson Murray, 1951
The Scottish Himalayan Expedition

Shortly after sunrise, my teammate Adam stepped out in front of our thirty-man assault force. Without a word, he began clearing a safe path or us to travel from our secure positions in a village we had cleared only an hour before, to a new cluster of buildings about a kilometer north. While the area we were leaving was free of Taliban fighters, weapons, and explosive hazards, the expectation was that we would encounter them all again on our transit to

Brad at U.S. Paralympics Trials in 2012

the new location. Despite knowing that his position in the patrol would be the first to encounter any of these threats, my teammate Adam did not hesitate to carry out his duty and find the safest path for our patrol to travel. He had done the same job every few days for the last eight months, and he knew that he was probably the most qualified person in the world to safely escort his team through the most dangerous place on earth. After leading the patrol nearly 400 meters or so, Adam came across one of his greatest fears—choke points.

Choke points caused by terrain and/or man-made structures are terrifying for EOD techs like Adam because they are prime locations for booby traps called IEDs (Improvised Explosive Devices). Before Adam was a small break in a wall, followed by a dried out irrigation ditch. Adam's first instinct was to avoid this area altogether, but, unfortunately, there was no other option. Adam had to face his greatest fear and find a seemingly nonexistent safe path through a lethal area. With his senses on high alert, and with the sure footing of a tightrope walker, Adam began to clear a path through the choke point. He identified a small but navigable route around what he assumed was the most hazardous part of the choke point, and he safely made it past the ditch, and began clearing a new path through the adjacent field. While clearing the new route, Adam frequently looked back to ensure that our patrol was able to follow the path he had cleared. After one such glance, Adam reassured himself that the path he had chosen was safe and passable, as three or four of his teammates were now safely across the ditch.

Then, just as he directed his gaze back toward the uncleared terrain in front of him, a deafening boom filled the air, and Adam was almost knocked over by a blast wave coming from behind him. Slightly confused and shocked, he looked back once again toward the patrol, and his stomach turned because he was no longer able to see our force. The choke point was now engulfed in a thick cloud of smoke making it impossible for anyone to see anything. After a moment that seemed a lot longer to Adam, but was only a few seconds, he deciphered that the fifth or sixth man back in the patrol had stepped out of his carefully cleared path, and had activated an IED. Adam shouted to the patrol to remain exactly where they were and to shift their gaze outward so that Taliban fighters would not be able to attack while the force was vulnerable.

Adam located the medic, an Air Force Pararescue Specialist, and began clearing a safe path back to one of the two severely injured members of the patrol. Once he got closer to the casualties, he was able to identify them as two of our Afghan soldiers, with whom we worked closely during all missions.

A moment later, I reached the choke point from my position in the middle of the patrol. I shouted to Adam something like, "What the hell happened?" He calmly described what he had seen, and we quickly divided up responsibility for the casualties. I was to safely escort the evacuation effort for the casualty who was lying in the blast site of the IED, while Adam would escort the evacuation effort for the casualty that had been thrown forward from the blast site.

After much struggle, I and two teammates, along with a few Afghans, safely removed the first casualty from the blast site to an area where the evacuation helicopter would land. I realized that a litter (a small foldable device used to carry the wounded) would make the evacuation of Adam's casualty much more manageable, and after a moment or two, I was able to locate one of the litters we routinely carried with our force. With it over my shoulder, I hurried to clear my way back towards Adam and the medic.

While on my way back through the choke point, I failed to identify a secondary IED that was sitting in close proximity to the device that had been activated a few moments earlier. As I stepped on an improvised pressure switch–not unlike the time pad placed at the end of a swimming lane, which stops the clock during a race–a circuit was connected, and the voltage stored in a nine-volt battery initiated a 40-pound explosion about four feet in front of me.

For a second time, Adam was alerted by the sound of a very close detonation, and this time he knew that I was the victim. He immediately heard me shouting to him, and he urged me to keep communicating, as it was the only way he could find my location through the new cloud of smoke. He quickly reached me, and began a hasty sweep of my body to determine the extent of the damage.

After determining that I was largely unharmed from the neck down, Adam grabbed me by the shoulder and exclaimed, "You look good man!!"

I replied, "My face hurts badly."

Adam responded, "Yeah, your face isn't pretty, but then again, it never was."

It was at that moment that I knew that everything was going to be fine. Adam's confidence and his poise under such dire circumstances gave me the courage and gumption to subdue my fears and participate in my own evacuation. With his support and that of a medic, I stood up and walked away from the blast site. Moments later, I boarded a helicopter that carried me away from the risks and hazards that Adam and my teammates still faced. They all had just witnessed three people maimed within inches of their lives, and they were now required to carry on as if nothing had happened. Teammates with the strength of character required to do that are incredibly rare, and I had the privilege of working with a force manned exclusively with men of such character.

The sun had not risen on my mother's small home in St. Petersburg, Florida. The sound of the phone ringing so early in the morning was certainly uncommon, so my mother answered skeptically as she wiped the sleep from her eyes. The slightly robotic tone of a voice bouncing via satellites across the atmosphere made the news seem all the more surreal. The description of the events that had occurred earlier that morning were both incredibly detailed and incredibly vague. Much of the message was lost on my mother; however, she did comprehend enough important details to instill in her both fear and hope. Her son had been badly injured, but was still alive. The major damage was to his face, and the extent was largely indeterminable. She was to pack her bags and await a phone call from a family outreach coordinator, who would provide details on how she was going to be flown to Bethesda Naval Hospital. She would meet me there once I was flown out of Afghanistan.

After what my mother describes as the longest three days of her life, she was able to meet me at the back of an ambulance near the loading docks of Bethesda Naval in Maryland. Accompanying her was my sister and one of my brothers, who had flown in from Kansas. Together, we began the longest six days of my life. For the first day of my stay at Bethesda, I was intubated, which means I had a tube inserted into my mouth that ran down my esophagus keeping an open airway. This was necessary to keep me breathing, but it took away my ability to speak. During my intubation, the only successful communication I made to my family was my use of a middle finger directed at my younger brother during a moment of frustration. Despite this, my family never skipped a beat, and never left my side.

Over the next few days, I went in and out of surgery countless times. The surgeries were aimed at healing the wounds on my face and potentially saving a small amount of vision that remained in my badly damaged eyes.

The adjustment from Afghanistan to the hospital was a difficult one for me at first, and it was compounded by the large quantity of pain-killing medication that I was consuming. I routinely said things that must have raised questions regarding my sanity. I jumped at the comforting touch of my family, and, at one point, I accused a nurse of conspiring to kidnap me from the hospital. Despite my crazy claims, and the gory details of surgery after surgery, my family was at my side, taking care of my every need. They never left me.

On the sixth day, surrounded by my family, four surgeons stood in my hospital room and described to me the last surgery that I would have to endure. During this surgery, the battered remains of my left eye would be removed, and the doctors would attempt to piece together the even more tattered remains of my right eye. After a lengthy description of the procedure,

I asked the doctors, "So in English, Doc, what are my chances...?" After a moment, choosing his words carefully, he replied, "You have a one to two percent chance of being able to perceive light with your right eye."

As the reality of the rest of my life set in, I hung my head. But in the same moment, I also wanted to be strong for my family who had been so strong for me. I looked at the doctors, or at least aimed my head in their general direction, smiled and said, "Well, I suppose that is better than a zero percent chance!"

The following day, after spending 12 hours in the operating room attempting to pull off a procedure that had never yet been performed successfully, the surgeons were forced to admit that they could not give me back any of the vision that I had lost the week earlier.

I thanked them for trying, and set my focus on my new goals: I will regain my independence, and I will regain the level of success that I had previously experienced. And finally, I will do it without the use of eyes.

Shortly after hearing news of my injury, my best friend Ian, stationed at the Navy's base on the Pacific Island of Guam, immediately, and without a second thought, submitted paperwork to use his saved days of leave in order to fly halfway around the world to be with me in the hospital. His parents, who effectively adopted me during our college years, as Ian and I made frequent surf trips to their home in Ventnor, New Jersey, also immediately coordinated their leave to join their son and me in the hospital.

Friends and acquaintances of mine flew, took trains, and drove from all corners of our great country to show their support and to be there for me during my time of need. All aspects of my chain of command from my previous teammates, to the Secretary of Defense, came by to wish me well, and to sincerely offer their assistance in any way I could imagine. The amount of love and support I received in the short period following my injury was the most inspiring experience I've had in my short life.

I felt undeserving of the commitment I received; however, I felt as though I had no choice but to reciprocate that commitment in the best way I knew how. I decided to use the love, support, and commitment that I received to help me muster the resolve and gumption to eliminate considering any possibility that my blindness would limit my potential in any way.

I owed it to all of those who had demonstrated unfailing commitment to me to get back to the person I had been as quickly as possible.

As a younger man I learned the concept of honor from my father. My virtues were strengthened by the lessons learned through my time in the military. My courage was put to the test on the battlefields of Iraq and Afghanistan. In the process, I learned the true meaning of brotherhood in the shared willingness to make sacrifice in the name of something greater than the individual or for another brother. Through personal adversity, I learned the true meaning of commitment.

Brad (right), with his brother Russell, receiving one of many gold medals in track at the Warrior Games in 2012

I am Brad Snyder. It is from the commitment of my friends and family that I now derive the strength and resolve to drive forward, manifest my own destiny, and seek out success in every avenue of my life.

A nation that makes a great distinction between its scholars and its warriors will have its laws made by cowards and its wars fought by fools.

—Thucydides
The History of the Peloponnesian War

In Our Conversations

Their Insights

During my conversations with the warriors, they shared more than their remarkable stories of survival. Clearly, their time spent in hospitals while recovering from war gave them plenty of opportunity to reflect on many aspects of courage, leadership, and military life.

I have summarized many of our conversations in order to fairly preserve their insights for you. Some of them are surprising, particularly their reflections on the enemy and on the need for civilians to better understand the military.

Should you want to hear them speak for themselves, you may listen to their comments by visiting Courage in America's Web site at: http://thecharacterbuildingproject.com/courage-in-america/.

On Courage and Leadership

In discussing courage and its role in leadership, Todd Nicely claims, "there are all kinds of courage." Steve Baskis ranks courage almost at the top of the qualities needed in a good leader, and Chad Ellinger concurs with its importance. However, Chad also highly rates other leadership qualities such as integrity, decisiveness, and faith as equally important for effectiveness. Sam Angert emphasizes the mental aspects of courage by describing a good leader as one who can boldly anticipate next moves as if he were virtually playing out a game of chess. Chase mentions that military leaders must show both mental and physical courage by overcoming the fact that all soldiers have a "spirit of fear." For Chase, focusing upon an important goal helps warriors to overcome fear. It empowers them to place themselves in danger for the good of a cause larger than themselves. Justin Constantine considers courage important beyond the battlefield as well. For him, it is a critical facet of effective leadership while in combat and is equally needed while recovering from traumatic injuries. Justin adds that, after battle, a wounded warrior must have the courage to "put himself out there" rather than "stay shuttered up inside." For example, Justin explains that it takes courage to identify one's weaknesses such as the effects of post-traumatic stress and to "seek the help needed." Todd sums the discussion up by stating courage requires leaders to "step outside their comfort zones" and "stand up for what is right." Brad Snyder believes, "the amount of courage utilized during combat has a direct correlation with the effectiveness of said leader."

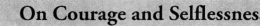

On Courage and Selflessness

In all the conversations with the wounded warriors, one common core value emerged: selflessness. Nothing gives another man courage more than another man's fear, or his injury. All talked about taking care of their military buddies by placing the good of the squad, unit, or group above their own needs. They claim they never did anything except what any of their buddies would have done in the same situation. No matter what nuance each brought to a definition of courage, they all agreed on one critical element: great leaders readily act for the good of others. At all times, they are willing to choose the "harder right" rather than the "easier wrong." For military leaders, selfless decision-making is the fruit of the virtue of courage, when exercised. This virtue is honed in all warriors by their culture, training them to focus first and foremost on the mission and achieve its goal at all cost. Failure is not an option.

Interestingly, the virtue of courage that all wounded warriors admired in their leaders is clearly evident in them as well. In fact, many displayed selflessness even before they enlisted in the military. Some felt called to respond to 9/11 and others to serve a noble cause. None spoke of joining the military because seething ambition drove them to advance their personal career. And after enlisting and being trained, each warrior willingly marched into the face of fear because they knew their fellow warriors shared their selfless values and would "have their back." Each devoted themselves to something larger than themselves.

On Courage in Battle

Courage is almost a contradiction in terms. It means a strong desire to live taking the form of a readiness to die. The best kind of courage for Steve Baskis is when an individual risks one's own life to save another. Steve does not believe courageous people confront more or less fear than people who lack courage. The difference is in how two persons manage a similar amount of fear. Steve believes people who are courageous push past the fear to accomplish something greater than them. For Steve, the courageous person could be acting without completely understanding the situation, it may be tiny pieces of fear all glued together propelling a person to take action.

Justin Constantine echoes Steve's view by relating the courage of Major Doug Zembiec, who, in his fourth tour in Iraq, was killed when leading a raid. Major Zembiec's quick thinking to re-orient his team's machine gun enabled the remaining members of his unit to accurately engage the primary source of the enemy's fire, saving the lives of his comrades.

Justin also sees opportunities to exhibit everyday courage outside the combat context. For example, he asks, "How many times do we hear a boss announce a concept that we think is wrong, or hear other people in our office make derogatory comments about someone else's belief system or ethnic/racial background? In each of these instances, it can take a lot of courage to voice your opinion and to correct these people."

Justin further explains where fear intersects with courage. "Courage relates to a person standing up to danger, fear, or intimidation in spite of his or her fear, and without any guarantee of success or survival. The fact that they are confronting whatever it is in front of them—whether it is an enemy in combat or a discriminatory company policy—shows their courage."

Chad Ellinger thinks of courage in terms of a victorious underdog. For Chad these kinds of stories seem to always exhibit how courage and timing can go hand in hand. Chad's favorite examples of courage involve restraint. Some of the most influential people in Chad's life demonstrated patience and were slow to make foolish decisions. The courage to "hold your fire" when things appear in disarray is a form of courageous defiance that many people lack. In Chad's opinion, the unspoken creed of courageous people is best captured by a quote of Ambrose Redmoon: "Courage is not the absence of fear, but the judgment that something else is more important than fear." A person with courage understands that overcoming fear associated with a courageous act is only a means to the end.

Sam Angert views courage as being instilled in military basic training and constantly was being reinforced by "following the reflection of the higher ranks." Perhaps the most basic expression of military-trained courage Sam believes is the determination to "leave no man behind." This theme of instinctively aiding a fallen comrade drives warriors to be courageous.

Chase Cooper agrees that the military slowly builds a warrior's confidence and courage through training. However, Chase goes to great length to show respect for the courage of the enemy. Chase notes that there are differing perspectives of courage, from our point of view as well as from the enemy's point of view. Although Chase disagrees with the extreme tactics of the enemy, he does grant it takes a certain type of courage to strap a bomb on yourself and detonate it. Chase is grateful for every courageous soldier from previous wars that have paved the way for today's soldiers to be safer and more effective.

Similar to a view expressed by Justin, Todd Nicely acknowledges courage outside the context of combat. Within the context of the Marines, Todd acknowledges being trained to perform as a unit, always remembering, "You are only as strong as your weakest link." Todd again speaks of the universal military understanding to never leave a man behind on the battlefield or in the rear. Todd admits of having run across few "ribbon chasers," but he warns that no one will succeed as a Marine if he or she is in it for individual glory.

For Brad Snyder, the best kind of courage is depicted when the Spartans utilized the fighting tactic of the phalanx the shield of a warrior protected the man standing beside him in formation, not necessarily himself. If a warrior failed to use his shield effectively he was putting his fellow-warrior at risk.

Whether or not courage began to develop in these warriors during their early family life, it is clear that their military training further cultivated this virtue. It prepared each to persevere and withstand danger in Iraq and Afghanistan and afterward.

On Courage vs. Selfishness

Conversation with the warriors took an interesting turn when the discussion questioned whether or not a warrior's actions could begin with the imperfect motive of selfishness and yet still be courageous.

Most would agree with the view of Steve Baskis when he clarifies, "It truly depends on the situation and experience of the individual involved." Sam Angert, Chase Cooper and Steve allow for instances when a selfish person can rise to the challenge and act courageously based on the immediate circumstances, for example, when his unit is under siege. They admit that exceptional circumstances can trigger a survival instinct even in a selfish person, which moves him or her to act courageously.

The three Marines interviewed: Chad Ellinger, Todd Nicely and Justin Constantine disagree. They seem to doubt that a selfish person can ever be truly courageous. "At the ripe old age of 33, I've yet to see it," states Chad.

Todd turns the focus around and describes the selfish nature of the enemy's tactics when they place roadside bombs and improvised explosive devices where children and other civilians are endangered. For Todd, this conduct is selfish and never courageous.

Justin, the practicing lawyer among the warriors, naturally examines motive when he distinguishes between the two ways to act. "Acting courageously includes within it a mindset of sacrifice for the greater good, while being selfish is more about personal survival."

Brad Snyder believes acts of courage can be inherently selfish. For example as a blind man, it takes a great deal of courage to overcome certain debilitating fears, but successfully overcoming those does not affect anyone else. Brad further clarifies his belief when "courageous acts are carried out at the benefit of another, then virtue is scaled positively."

All speak to the inspiring example of courage that was exhibited on 9/11 when New York firefighters raced unselfishly and courageously into the flaming Twin Towers to rescue those trying to escape the crumbling debris. All believe, whether it is by learning the "Soldiers Creed," or by studying the history of the Marine Corps, that courage can be taught and bred from the military culture. The group claims that warriors learn courage by modeling their conduct on the great warriors who have courageously gone into combat before them. It is their legacy of honor, courage and commitment—the core values of a hero—that teach today's generation of warriors to be selfless. And all the warriors also agree on one final point: that courage is the most beneficial character trait a warrior can possess.

On Courage in the Enemy

Somewhat unique to the wars of this century is the sad fact that a disproportionate number of the traumatic injuries received have come from improvised explosive devices (IEDs). Since most of the warriors interviewed were seriously injured by them, it was of interest to ask whether or not they consider use of such sinister devices courageous? Given the severity of injuries inflicted upon them by IEDs, there is a surprising lack of bitterness in their responses.

Chad Ellinger answered by offering more of an analysis of the tactics of the enemy. He explained:

> "During combat, I acknowledged my opponent's skill and tactics. I wanted to know everything about their motivations, so I could exploit any weaknesses. I'm sure a civilian observer might identify several differences between me and the enemy, but today I'm choosing not to search my soul to find any."

Justin Constantine saw a surprising amount of similarity between himself and his enemy in combat when it comes to motivation to fight. He explains his thoughts this way:

> "I would say Marines and terrorists have a lot in common. They both fervently believe in what they are doing and are committed to their cause. They both have enemies they are trying to defeat. They both will go to great lengths to accomplish their missions, and they both have support from many people in their home countries and around the world. Of

course, there are also a lot of distinctions between Marines and terrorists, but I believe that it is definitely possible for terrorists to be courageous; especially in the way we commonly use the term. We may hate what terrorists do, and the harm they commit, but that is irrelevant. There are plenty of people around the world who would characterize us as terrorists—it is all in the eye of the beholder."

With a measured response, Steve Baskis explains that love of country is global. He declares:

"I understand things with my thinking colored by the environment in which I grew up. I believe that you could draw similarities between courage shown by the enemy and American service members. I am a human being who has lived in one part of the world–the United States– and has grown to love that country. I am a person who has been taught to love and respect certain things, but I could say the same for the enemy about his country. We are both trying to accomplish some patriotic goal or objective in the end."

Todd Nicely had less sympathy for an enemy "who hides behind women and children and deploys IED's in places that put their own civilians at risk for mortal injury." He would not consider that act courageous.

And Sam Angert, the only Jewish soldier in his entire brigade, had to endure the enemy's public denigration of the state of Israel, shows no bitterness. He offers the briefest opinion on the subject. He declares that on all sides of battle, warriors learn that "life is very precious."

Brad Snyder's view, based on a definition of courage as the conquering of a fear, the "actions of a terrorist could absolutely be considered courageous." Brad does grant a certain degree of respect be given to an adversary who is willing to give his life for the cause he or she believes in. However, Brad makes a distinction for the "justness of the cause for which we fight." Brad states, "We fight to protect the lives, liberties, and the pursuit of happiness of both our countrymen and for those around the world."

Our conversations about courage on both sides of battle seem to capture our warriors' respect for an opponent's patriotism when the fight remains between military targets, but a major distinction between good guys and bad guys occurs when they use civilians as human shields instead of making themselves the human shields.

There is a striking contrast in maturity when these heroes who have returned from war to rebuild their young injured bodies are compared to their college-age counterparts. Clearly, in many cases, war accelerates character development in young men and women. Several characterized their civilian contemporaries as immature. For example, Sam Angert thinks that many of his contemporaries feel entitled. Chase Cooper observes that many of them appear aimless, lack a strong work ethic, and seem unwilling to sacrifice for others.

Steve Baskis, Justin Constantine and Chad Ellinger acknowledge a perception problem. While the military is not for all citizens, appreciation for what the military does should be for all. Civilian exposure to our nation's military men and women needs to be improved. Many returning warriors could speak to civilian audiences about their military experience as a way to bridge the gap.

Steve believes the skills and experiences he gained while serving were invaluable to him. Steve volunteered because he believed "by serving he would make a difference in the world." Steve noted it is "hard for some people to realize and understand certain things if they have not lived or experienced war. War puts things in perspective. Veterans alone can share this knowledge."

Justin adds that, "There are a number of things civilians can learn from members of the military. They range from how to present oneself (we are all taught to speak respectfully, stand tall, exercise regularly, walk with our shoulders back and to have a command presence), to the importance of teamwork (everything we do is as part of a team, and people from all races and beliefs are made to train and work together), and to understanding that sacrifice is part of service and that our individual needs are not the most important consideration."

Chad was struck by the high expectations he perceived from civilians after his military career ended and he rejoined them in the private sector: "Within a professional setting, I've worked with several people who were not part of the military, and they all seemed to have unspoken expectations of a former military member. They had a common belief that the military conducts itself in the most professional way possible." Yet Chad still acknowledges a wide gap in civilian perception of the military. "To a large extent, the civilian population remains disconnected from understanding everything the military does on their behalf."

Although Todd Nicely admits the "civilian culture might be more self-centered, than the spirit he witnessed in the Marine Corps." Todd qualifies that "There are those in both civilian and military life who want to do good." Todd believes, "It is the level of training received by those in the military that upgrades and hones the values that recruits bring into, and out of, the military."

Brad says, "It is imperative that the people of the United States realize and appreciate the daily sacrifice of service members on their behalf. There are hundreds of thousands, if not millions of citizens of the U.S. who are willing to make the ultimate sacrifice for our way of life, yet that number is less than one percent of the overall population of the United States. I believe a large contingent of our population is blissfully unaware of the terrible things that happen outside our borders, and the nefarious characters who wish to do us harm."

Overall, the warriors are grateful to have left a culture of self-gratification and be trained in a culture of accountability, self-discipline and sacrifice. If civilians–including our politicians–could have the opportunity to learn from our returning military men and women, maybe our country could experience a revival of an ethic of selfless teamwork. Then perhaps the gap between our military and civilian cultures could shrink.

In Their Own Voices: Their Podcasts

To listen to several recorded conversations with the wounded warriors, please visit Courage in America's Web site at:

http://thecharacterbuildingproject.com/courage-in-america/

You can hear Sam Angert explain his distinctions between physical and moral courage at:

http://thecharacterbuildingproject.com/warriors/sam-angert/
sam-angert-interview/

Steve Baskis provides a thoughtful reflection upon the fine line between courage and foolishness depending upon the circumstances. Read about his take on courage at:

http://thecharacterbuildingproject.com/warriors/steve-baskis/
steve-baskis-interview/

Justin Constantine points out that it takes courage after war to do a self-assessment and request the help needed:

http://thecharacterbuildingproject.com/warriors/
justin-constantine/justin-constantine-interview/

Chase Cooper explains that courage is simply being ready to doing what needs to be done and it can be taught and even learned from others around you:

http://thecharacterbuildingproject.com/warriors/chase-cooper/
chase-cooper-interview/

Chad Ellinger thinks that at times courage can show itself as restraint. Read his thoughts at:
http://thecharacterbuildingproject.com/warriors/chad-ellinger/chad-ellinger-interview/

Todd Nicely's tells the incredible story of the courage it took to rebuild his life after losing both arms and both legs in battle:
http://thecharacterbuildingproject.com/warriors/todd-nicely/todd-nicely-interview/

Brad Snyder harkens back to Spartan mothers who would tell their sons as they marched off to battle, "Come back with your shield, or upon it.":
http://thecharacterbuildingproject.com/warriors/bradley-snyder/bradley-snyder-interview/

Courage is reckoned the greatest of all virtues; because, unless a man has that virtue, he has no security for preserving any other.

—Samuel Johnson
The Life of Samuel Johnson
by James Boswell

In Response to Their Courage

There is something striking about the attitude present in the military hospitals where our nation's heroes are recovering. The spirit is captured by General Peter Pace, a retired United States Marine Corps general who served as the 17th Chairman of the Joint Chiefs of Staff, the first Marine appointed to the United States' highest-ranking military office. His quote is visible in many hospital rooms of the wounded warriors:

> "There are those who speak about you who say, 'He lost an arm, he lost a leg, she lost her sight.' I object. You gave your arm. You gave your leg. You gave your sight. As gifts to your nation. That we might live in freedom. Thank you. And to your families. Families of the fallen and families of the wounded. You sacrificed in ways that those of us who have not walked in your shoes can only imagine."

Indeed, I can not possibly comprehend their sacrifices and am amazed at the ability of these young volunteers to muster their courage when needed. The die is cast once a warrior is wounded.

Many virtues honed during the earlier years of their lives, including the courage that led them to volunteer to fight for our country, come to center stage and are tested. In each case, the long list of the extent of injury is matched first by great stamina and physical courage. Then several other character traits become evident: resoluteness, diligence, duty, service, honor, loyalty, and valor. Many of the traits that were cultivated in preparation for battle sustain them through the battle for their own life. All would agree not letting fear hold them back, was the choice each made to living the most rewarding life possible. A key trait that the wounded warriors who make a successful recovery seem to share is the ability to channel their intensity into something larger and more enduring than themselves. That something can be love of country, of family, of loyal friends, of fellow-military, of God, but it will not be love of self, or brooding over self.

It would be negligent to not mention courage in the families of the injured. Family courage is also a major contributor to the successful recovery of wounded warriors. Walter Reed National Military Medical Center in Bethesda teems with the unconditional love among family members as they rally around the wounded warriors. Entire families exhibit their selfless loyalty and duty toward their warrior as all endure and build the willpower needed to meet the long rehabilitation challenges ahead. This behavior is remarkable when one considers that the families did not volunteer to put their lives at risk. (They may not even have supported a family member's choice to join the military.) They just assemble with little notice to pick up the pieces. The selflessness exhibited by families of the wounded even goes beyond their loved ones as many reach out to the fellow-wounded with encouragement and support. Their courage is exceptional.

It was Walter Lippmann who said, "He has honor if he holds to an ideal of conduct though it is inconvenient, unprofitable or dangerous to do so." At a time in our country when there is a diminished sense of morality and idealism, we can learn much from these honorable wounded warriors who are returning from war and from the families that help the injured to rebuild their lives. They are truly men and families of honor.

But we can do more than just learn from our troops. I invite many of you to join me in finding new ways to support the nation's wounded warriors, because our military heroes and their families deserve our help and should never be forgotten. Please visit the Courage in America Web site at: http://thecharacterbuilding-project.com/courage-in-america/ to find financially responsible charities that support our wounded military men and women. No contribution is too small when it touches the hearts of the injured.

About the Author

I am a blessed man. I enjoy life with my loving wife of 44 years. Together we are the proud parents of three lawyers from the University of Virginia. All our children survived our parenting, married well, albeit to more lawyers, and graced our ever-expanding clan with twelve beautiful and talented grandchildren.

My 30-plus year career in the tough advocacy business in Washington, D.C., is now winding down, so I have chosen to spend my newly discovered free time helping wounded warriors and veterans as they return home after 11 years of war. Their needs are great on many fronts. My small contribution will be to profile individual warriors and help transition them into meaningful civilian lives.

Thanks to the initiatives of several close buddies from the United States Marine Corps as well as of the United States Special Operations Command, I have been afforded the privilege of visiting Mologne House and the new Walter Reed National Medical Center where I have met warriors with traumatic brain injuries (TBI) and many single, double, triple, and quadruple amputees who "work out" there at the Military Assistance Training Center (MATC). I have witnessed these young heroes demonstrating extraordinary courage while dealing with the rigors of the painful rehabilitation necessary to get them out of their chairs and up on prosthetics. They are America's finest… Airmen, Ranger's, Seals, Delta guys, Soldiers and Marines. Visit after visit, I see the true grit of these warriors, I witness them pushing through the adversity of their pain and injuries without complaining or playing the victim card.

My first book, *Politics with Principle: Characters with Character* demonstrated that several virtues actually exist in politics in our country. With the publication of *Courage in America: Warriors with Character,* I offer yet another demonstration of extraordinary virtue. This time the virtue is the courage that is exhibited by our country's military, particularly by our wounded warriors and their families.

Each night I remember the wounded warriors and their families on my beads. I pray for their successful physical rehabilitation and for all efforts to help them transition into civilian lives. I also hope that I can somehow capture their heroism and offer it as inspiration and hope for others who will face similar traumatic injuries in the future.

To meet many of our country's wounded American military heroes and discover ways you can help them, too, please visit the Character Building Project at: http://thecharacterbuildingproject. com/courage-in-america/

Also by
Michael J. Kerrigan

Politics with Principle: Ten Characters with Character by Michael J. Kerrigan

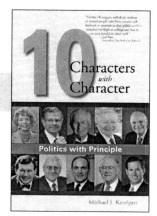

Politics with Principle: Ten Characters with Character validates the belief that it is possible for public servants to achieve success in the political arena without lying, cheating, or stealing along the way. It is the author's hope that this book will deepen the reader's appreciation for all in political life who conduct themselves honorably as well as encourage future aspirants of good character to consider public service. This book shows a rising generation the extent to which their own future will depend on the character traits they build in the present. By studying the exemplary characters showcased within, students of politics will be able to imitate their virtuous habits of life, thought, and action.

Today public cynicism about government officials is very high. Michael Kerrigan's well-done analysis of several people who have served with distinction reminds us that public service remains our highest calling and that it can and should be done well.

—*Joel Klein, Chancellor, New York City Schools, New York, NY*

Michael Kerrigan is a longtime friend and has great insight into the functioning of government, history, and our leaders. He has great appreciation for the need of moral, disciplined leadership not only to lead but also to set examples for generations to come. It is in stark contrast to the comment "they are all crooks" and the cynicism that is so prevalent today. Many of our leaders are individuals with outstanding principles and character, which is seldom reported but greatly needed for our country to excel. Thanks to Michael we can gain insight and learn from some of them.

—*Don Nickles, former United States Senator, Oklahoma*

ISBN: 978-1-60494-447-1 paperback • ISBN: 978-1-60494-448-8 hardcover
ASIN: B0045Y1O4I Kindle edition • at Amazon.com and other online bookstores

CPSIA information can be obtained at www.ICGtesting.com
Printed in the USA
BVOW080037121212

307881BV00005B/10/P